The Pattern of SOVIET POWER

Books by EDGAR SNOW

FAR EASTERN FRONT

LIVING CHINA

RED STAR OVER CHINA

THE BATTLE FOR ASIA

PEOPLE ON OUR SIDE

THE PATTERN OF SOVIET POWER

*

The Pattern of
SOVIET
POWER

by Edgar Snow

RANDOM HOUSE

NEW YORK

THIS IS A RANDOM HOUSE WARTIME BOOK

IT IS MANUFACTURED UNDER EMERGENCY CONDITIONS AND COMPLIES WITH THE GOVERNMENT'S REQUEST TO CONSERVE ESSENTIAL MATERIALS IN EVERY POSSIBLE WAY.

First Printing

61885

327.47

S674p

MANUFACTURED IN THE UNITED STATES OF AMERICA

To

BEN HIBBS *and*
MARTIN SOMMERS

*who gave me this assign-
ment and full freedom to
report it.*

Contents

Chapter One

LONG BRIGHT DAYS

Chapter Two

STALIN ENTERS THE BALKANS

Chapter Three

POLISH INTERLUDE

Chapter Four

RED STAR OVER EASTERN EUROPE

Chapter Nine

STALIN AT WAR

Chapter Ten

MEN OF THE KREMLIN

Chapter Eleven

RUSSIA REDISCOVERS HER PAST

Chapter Twelve

THE PARTY AND THE PEOPLE

List of Illustrations

xi

The Pattern of SOVIET POWER

CHAPTER ONE

Long Bright Days

·◦[I]◦·

I

Back to Moscow

WHEN I had left Moscow early in 1943, near the end of a tense and anxious winter, it was still a place of hunger and suffering beneath its hard determination, and behind the dark ice-coated buildings which lined its shabby streets. People had little to cheer them then except the fresh triumph at Stalingrad, the hope of a western front in Europe, and the warm urge of spring in the air. The front was not far off and Moscow lay under threat of siege and what would prove to be the last great German offensive, coming out of Orel. A year had gone by and it was already difficult to believe these were the same Muscovites. They seemed to wear new faces full of hope and confidence, and the city was radiant with light in contrast to the memory I had carried around the world with me.

Summer accounted for some of the changed aspect, of course. All around for a thousand miles or more I saw, flying up from Astrakhan, an endless expanse of vivid green, as lush and smiling with crops as in winter it was forbidding and deathlike in its still mask of white, charred by the deep gloomy forests of birch. Now everything in Moscow seemed newly washed, even the air, and this was not just summer illusion. The drapery of painted trees and factories and apartment buildings had been scrubbed from the Kremlin buildings and walls, so that now they have dimensions again, and form and color. The Bolshoi Theater had taken off its scaffoldings and its fine columns sparkled in the

3

blessed sun. Now you could see that the University and Chaikovsky Hall and a dozen other buildings were really very good, something you never noticed when tricks of camouflage confused the eye, and the stinging wind kept your face buried low in a fur collar.

So Russia really had color, and not only in daylight. After the long dusk there was almost always a salute for new victories. Throngs of lightly clad women and a scattering of soldiers gathered on the twilit streets, in Red Square, on the bridge across the Moscow River below the Kremlin towers, on Comintern Square and in Revolutionary Plaza before the Metropole. All over Moscow people waited for the fireworks. Now it was all reverse traffic for Hitler. His armies were being ground to pieces under triumphant offensives in the Ukraine, in White Russia, in the Baltic States. Nothing could save him now, and Moscow knew it. Guns thundered every night, and red, yellow and green rockets wove bright patterns against the northern stars. Radio loudspeakers blared forth the new Soviet anthem on the streets, and the names of heroes of the day were read to the listening nation. The Voice of Moscow that broadcast them was no calmer, no more nor less hurried, than when it had been obliged to announce "Citizens, Moscow is under attack."

Among the watchers before the Metropole stood Jack Margolis, the dark little British-born manager of the hotel, who married a Russian girl a decade ago and gave up his British passport to become a Soviet citizen. Now he was glad again that he had done so. "Look at it," he exclaimed, and a grin effaced his old sadness. "It's just like before the war. Look at the crowds—it's peace again! Oh, it's great to be a *Russian* these days!"

Behind him, the Metropole had become the scene of bitter competition for rooms. Correspondents were no longer the small tight band of a year ago and the male monopoly had been broken by the arrival of indefatigables like Anna Louise Strong and Ella Winter. Rivalry for space was further intensified by the overflow from the swollen embassies as new diplomats came in, demand-

ing priorities, and representatives appeared from half-forgotten
countries preparing for rebirth. Nobody yet knew what it was
going to mean when Russia became the only great power in
Europe, but every Government now realized the need to have
more and more men here to study what Churchill had called "a
riddle wrapped in an enigma." And soon Winston himself would
come to join the seekers after answers.

The British Ministry of Information had lodged a large staff
in the Metropole; various military and diplomatic missions had
sealed off blocks of rooms for their own use; and on top of that
American engineers and fur buyers were back demanding ac-
commodations. What was happening here was going on at every
other hotel and all over the city. It was almost impossible to get
a bed anywhere. This city had had four million inhabitants before the war; during the evacuation it had dropped to half that;
and now it was back with more Muscovites than ever.

Houses and apartment buildings were disintegrating more
rapidly than the Metropole. *Pravda* took time out from telling
the Allies what was wrong on the western front, to issue warnings to bewildered citizens to get on with the apparently impossible. "There are no special insurmountable circumstances,"
Pravda pundits complacently asserted, "standing in the way.
And if in some cities things are in bad shape, if roofs leak, if plas-
ter falls down, if repairing is done badly, it's the fault of local
governmental and party bodies."

Paint, materials, transportation, the labor question—those
weren't problems for *Pravda* to solve. It was "up to the party
bodies."

Everywhere now people were more concerned with hum-
drum domestic and household needs than in the leaner days of
war. There was more grumbling; the city was no longer holding
its breath. Any country is far more dramatic in time of defeat
and mounting disaster than it is in days of victory, and if Moscow at first seemed a happier place, it was a less exciting one.
The Government would have to invoke more than patriotism to

impart to the prosaic tasks that lay ahead the heroic stamp that had called forth the best in every Russian during the crisis of his nation's existence.

II

Prices—and Prices

ONE of the most puzzling things about Russia, however, is that while its bureaucrats bungle a hundred simple tasks, or neglect an easily remedied nuisance till it becomes a serious menace, just when you decide that nothing can be going right, where such glaring inefficiency prevails, you are astonished by revelation of some major accomplishment requiring a high degree of organization and foresight. This paradox is what made people speak of "miracles" being achieved during the war. In matters that really counted, not only on the fast-moving front but in the growing pace of production and in rehabilitation work in the devastated areas, things were still happening in that big, unexpected, deceptive Russian way.

The year's triumphs at the front, for example, were well matched in the rear by the truly magnificent success of the women and children of the reoccupied Ukraine and White Russia in bringing in a bountiful harvest. On those black plains, which before the war alone produced almost a third of the nation's wheat crop, obstacles as serious as German defense works confronted the Soviets. Seed grain was largely gone; thousands of combines and harvesters had been wrecked or carried away; few cattle remained; and literally millions of men had perished or been driven west.

Yet somehow the land was cultivated and planted and the crop reaped, while villages and towns still lay in ashes. "I don't know how they've done it," a Frenchman just back from a trip through the Ukraine told me, "but it's a fact that everywhere I went the fields were covered with glorious crops. From the best estimates I could get it will be a rich yield—eighty to ninety percent of a normal year." Later on I had an opportunity to find out, on the spot, how the effort had been organized—a story of the "bitter strength" of Russia told elsewhere in this book.

Optimism over the Ukrainian harvest had apparently influenced the food commissariats, and people were getting a little more to eat. Norms of rationed food had not increased, but stores more often were able to supply the minimum guaranteed. All over Russia well-stocked "commercial" food stores were opening. Mostorg, the capital's big department store, had reopened with shelves bulging with goods, and a number of variety shops were offering articles to the general public for the first time since 1941.

The so-called commercial stores were, of course, state-owned and operated. Unlike establishments which provided goods only for ration coupons and at controlled, pre-war prices, the former sold everything at inflated prices, in competition with the black market. Commercial stores were thus an interesting demonstration of how state control of trade could be manipulated for multiple purposes. In this case they were a morale builder, for they hinted of a return to normality. Also, they were an anti-inflation measure; they neatly extracted inflation rubles from the over-stuffed pockets of speculators and peasants. They gradually forced the black market down, until it would ultimately disappear.

Butter and sugar already cost less than half the 1943 prices and potatoes were down more than sixty percent. In general, consumers' goods prices were being reduced about ten percent every month. But they were still fantastically high compared to pre-war and rationed prices. In 1944 a pound of white bread in the commercial stores still cost $10, figured at the official exchange rate of five rubles to the dollar. Sugar cost 350 rubles a pound, or $70, and butter about the same. But in the "limited" or rationed-goods shops sugar was only three rubles a pound, and butter only fourteen rubles, and as foreigners got a special diplomatic rate of twelve rubles to the dollar, such prices were not exorbitant—for us.

Correspondents were allowed the same food norms as diplomats and it was very generous—far more than one person could eat. You had the choice of three meals a day at the Metropole, and a small additional ration at the diplomatic store, or of eating one, two or no meals at the hotel, and buying the balance in unprepared foods. Like most correspondents I took the store rations for the equivalent of breakfast and supper, and ate only the midday meal, which the Russians call dinner, at the Metropole. This gave me, monthly, thirty-six pounds of bread, six pounds of sugar, six pounds of meat and six of fish, nearly six pounds of butter and cheese, thirty pounds of potatoes, four cakes of soap (which on the open market cost 100 rubles a bar), and a long list of odds and ends, including four litres of vodka and wine. One Metropole dinner alone was more than the average Russian got in a couple of days, so that all that extra bounty enabled the correspondent to play good Samaritan or host to such Russians as could be enticed into acquaintance with a foreigner.

It was a reasonable arrangement, however, because when you bought anything outside the hotel or the special stores, you were robbed. My first night at the Bolshoi Theater I saw *Prince Igor*, a magnificent opera, and under the spell of this lavish production I took a friend into the restaurant, between acts, and ordered tea and eclairs. The check was the equivalent of $48. Outside the theater, columns of civilians waited for a chance to buy Russian Eskimo pies, considered a bargain at $6 a pie.

In some of the new commercial cafés and restaurants there

was music, and in the fashionable Moscow Hotel there was
dancing with Svassman's American-style swing band. I was
going to invite a party of four people to supper there one night
to celebrate a certain occasion, but took the precaution of asking, in advance, the cost of a four-course meal, with two bottles
of champagne. The maitre d'hôtel figured it out at 3,105 rubles,
sans tip, or about $600, at five to one. I settled for a home-cooked
meal in the Metropole instead.

Still, the Moscow Hotel was always crowded with officers and
officials and a certain number of demi-mondes who seemed attached to the place. Red Army officers and privileged bureaucrats, distinguished intellectual and war and labor heroes were
given special books entitling them to discounts of from ten to
sixty percent at all state stores, as well as in theaters and hotels.
Officers on leave after months at the front came in like the old
miners to Dawson, their pockets bulging with cash and loaded
for b'ar. But even for the citizen with no surplus rubles all the
gay windows filled with foods and wine, the shops reopened,
and cafés flourishing, meant at least that peace was slowly ebb-
ing back.

Life was growing a little easier in other respects. In the factories a few elderly people were getting vacations with pay
again, and the new law promised mothers a longer maternity
leave. More skilled workers, teachers, engineers and other specialists were being released by the Army. Now it was possible to
travel as far as 140 kilometers outside the capital, without military permits; suburban trains were frequent, and surprisingly
punctual. Every factory and every institution seemed to have its
dacha, or summer cabin, and thousands flocked to the country
every week-end, half bent on serious work and half on holiday.
Amateur gardeners had contributed enormously to declining
prices and most people were able to lay in some stock of vegetables for the winter ahead.

What astonished me was how few signs of malnutrition you

saw on the streets: an occasional bandy-legged boy, some ema-
ciated old people. But they were lost in the impression you got
from the rugged youth everywhere, especially the bare hard-
muscled legs of Russian women. How they managed to keep so
much flesh on their bodies, on a diet of cabbage soup and black
bread, continued to baffle me. There was an All-Union Sports
Parade at the Moscow Dynamo, and hardly a seat was vacant in
the huge stadium, which holds 60,000. It was an unusual kind of
meet because all the competitors were members of athletic clubs
attached to factories and Soviet institutions—muscular but over-
age or exempt men and women ranging from girls in their 'teens
to middle-aged mothers. Their skirtless blue-and-white sports
tights clung to them like postage stamps. It was a frank display
of healthy vigorous bodies and left you with the impression of a
nation still holding back boundless reserves of power, un-
touched by the war.

In my own mind those athletic workers formed a contrast
with the 60,000 gray, grizzled, beaten Germans who were led
next day between rows of millions of onlookers lining the streets.
It was a strangely quiet, well-behaved crowd that watched them.
As in Leninsk, where I had been when German prisoners taken
at Stalingrad were marched through, the Muscovites made no
demonstration, did not shout, hiss nor spit curses at them. Instead, now and then you heard an old woman say, "Look at that
young one there; the fellow has no shoes," or remark quietly,
"Take a good look at Moscow, Fritz—after all, you got here at
last, though not quite the way Hitler promised you." Now and
then the German soldiers—led off by a dozen Prussian generals
still haughty and wearing their decorations—stole furtive glances
up the canyon of big solid buildings on Gorky Street, looking for
signs of that "obliterated" Moscow which Goebbels boasted the
Luftwaffe had achieved many months earlier.

Before their march through town some of the prisoners had
been quartered at the big Moscow race track. The town fathers

hastened to fumigate it when their guests had departed. Not long afterward the papers advertised that the usual annual trotting races were to be held. I went out with Alex Werth, of the *Times* (London), and Marjorie Shaw of the *Mirror,* and the enchanting Mrs. Colombo, just to make sure it wasn't a gag. The races came off, all right, attended by Moscow's equivalent of the international smart set, wearing linen hats and dusters, and equipped with field-glasses and tips on the favorites. All the Best People were there, looking unpressed and seedy, but as absorbed in the races as a crowd of Kentucky colonels.

It was a memorable day for two reasons, besides the company. Alex and I made a bet and cleared fifty rubles after paying the state tax. The other reason was that a band marched in, mounted a stand set in the middle of the field, and played the *International.* It was the only time I heard the former Soviet national anthem, which was abandoned after the dissolution of the Comintern, all the time I was in Russia. Nor had anyone else I questioned later heard it played in public since the ban. I never could see the connection with the trotting races, myself. Perhaps the horses are being encouraged to unite, they had nothing to lose . . .

Not many people realize how the Soviet Government found its new anthem. A nation-wide contest was held, and virtually every composer contributed an offering. After many weeks the judges narrowed down the favorites to a few, which were finally played for Stalin and the Politburo. After hearing them all, the party chieftains were undecided. In the end no composer's entry was chosen. The big shots solved the matter by adopting the old party song as the new anthem—and taking over the old *International* as the new party song. Dinned into the citizen's ears from loudspeakers every day, the new hymn won speedy acceptance. It has dignity, power and grandeur. Like "bourgeois" anthems, too, it is quite impossible to sing.

III

War and Art

"From now on life can only become better," a Russian optimist explained to me. "We have known the worst; so there's nothing but good lying ahead. A few more pounds of potatoes a month, an extra kilo of sugar, our own vegetables from our own gardens—these things are marks of real progress for us. For Germany the cost of the war is just beginning. For us—the price has about been paid."

That wasn't strictly correct, of course. Casualties of the summer offensive hadn't yet been announced and the Red Army's swift advances were not cheaply made. What it would mean to Russia to get along with ten to fifteen million fewer able-bodied men had yet to be fully realized. I thought of that often when from my window in the hotel, overlooking Sverdlovsk Plaza and the Bolshoi, I saw on the streets increasing numbers of cripples mingling with the crowds. Every day at a certain hour two tow-headed children led across the busy traffic a blind young man back from the war. He was still paying the price for Russia's victory and would go on paying, with millions of others, for the rest of his life.

The long bright summer days are so few in Moscow that the end of every one of them carries the regret of a farewell. One of the days when I dropped everything for that sun that wouldn't keep I went out to Gorky Park of Culture and Rest and walked miles along the Moscow River, exploring the hills and ravines. In one corner of the park there was a big exhibit of captured

12

enemy war trophies: tanks and guns and planes from every
arsenal of Europe—German stuff, and Czech, Italian, Austrian,
French, Belgian, Polish, even Spanish. It gave you the feeling,
as it was probably intended to do, that Hitler had really struck
Russia with all Europe mobilized behind him and serving his
purpose. In a way more eloquent than words it told you why the
Red Army, when it entered Berlin, would insist on a Europe in
which that couldn't happen again.

Walking or hopping or stumping in between the rows of tanks,
or somehow scrambling up and down the little hills, were groups
of white-clad, crippled veterans. There was the clear exchange
before you, an arm or a leg or a piece of skull missing from each
of these men, as the cost of the trophies taken from the enemy;
and for every three cripples, one dead comrade. All these wrecks
came from near-by hospitals and this was now their playground;
you wondered what Russia would look like when they were all
turned back onto the country. It was a thing to remember, these
armless and legless youths with old faces who had hardly looked
on life, lining the river bank, silently watching the shouting
young boys and girls gaily swimming or boating below them.
Sometimes they hung together and sang their songs of battle
and their confidence seemed to flow back and they gazed at the
civilians with proud contempt.

This army would bind up but not forget its wounds, you
knew, when it returned. The finest manhood and some of the
ablest leadership were still in uniform, still inarticulate in society, as in our own country. When you remembered that Soviet
organizations had fulfilled all the tasks assigned them despite
that handicap, you had to conclude that the performance would
improve when the surviving males came back to their jobs. For
a long time their influence would be felt as apart from those who
did not fight in the trenches—yet no one knew quite how they
would assert themselves.

What was happening below the surface in the Army, and
what was fermenting in the civilian mind? How many of the

wartime improvisations would be permanently incorporated
into the Soviet system and into the post-war reading of Marxism?
The answers weren't readily available, but it was fascinating to
speculate about the phenomena you could see around you.

Take the Soviet theater. Virtually all the plays of the past season, and those coming, had little to do with Communism as an
ideology. Many were based on literary classics produced in
"bourgeois" or feudal societies. The most popular play of the
season was *The Road to New York*, adapted from the American
movie hit *It Happened One Night*. Among productions announced for autumn none seemed to deal with living contro-
versial political questions—which could or could not be a reflection of the noncommittal state of the Soviet mind.

Hamlet and *Othello* were featured. Several classics by Os-
trovski, who died sixty years ago, and Goncharov, who was born
the year Kutuzov met Napoleon at Borodino, were being revived. Both authors were aristocrats. Where were the plays of
poets and playwrights the Government had been financing all
during the war? If Soviet industry had been no more produc-
tive, where would the Red Army be?

There was a return to all classics in literature, too. On the for-
tieth anniversary of the death of Anton Chekhov, whom some
Russian Communists once ridiculed as a bourgeois artist, memorial meetings were held everywhere, streets were renamed
for him, new monuments were ordered erected. Most papers
devoted fully half their scant space to eulogizing Chekhov. So
the glorification of nineteenth-century Russian art and literature, stimulated for patriotic reasons during the war, seemed
likely to increase in the after-war.

For the first time in Soviet history the theater was offering
Oscar Wilde to the public. *The Ideal Husband* had been chosen
for reasons not easily discernible in the newspaper white-space
between the lines, where some people claimed to do their most
assiduous reading. One night I asked a party of Russian intellectuals why the ultra-bourgeois Wilde should be unearthed at

this particular moment and in such a piece of apparently irrelevant dilettantism.

"Because it's droll," a poet answered, "and at the end of war in any country people want a certain amount of distraction. With us Russians our tragedy is never far away from comedy and the ridiculous—and vice versa. You have escapist art in America, too, haven't you?"

Another writer suggested that *The Ideal Husband* was being done because it portrayed the behavior of some well-bred English people and fully vindicated the stability of the home. One evening when I talked to Sofia Andreyevna Tolstoy, Count Leo's granddaughter, who now runs all the Tolstoy museums in Russia, she spoke of a tremendous interest among all young people in practically every Russian classical writer of the past two centuries. She told also of the avid search for all kinds of English literature in Moscow. In the many second-hand bookshops it was almost impossible to buy an English book, and English dictionaries or grammars were scarcer than silk hose.

The hunger for knowledge of English and American culture was far greater than at any time in Russian history. Now that the western front had been opened, the Russians could frankly express their interest and I seldom met one who knew English who didn't plead for something to read. Before the war the Russians had always had a certain respect for German culture, but little of that was surviving now except a reverence for German music, and for Goethe. Seen from Moscow, England and France were all that was left of continental culture, the only sources from which Russian intellectuals felt they could draw new inspiration. They deeply sensed the need for enriching their own literature by opening new doors to England.

Young Russians were taking an extraordinary interest in good manners and other matters involving what was formerly dismissed by the party as "petty personal relationships." One of my Russian friends had recently translated an old English book on etiquette, which instructed readers not to make noises when eating, not to cough and spit on the floor, not to knock ladies down to get through a door first, and not to fight in public. It was selling like peanuts. Soon you won't be able to tell a man's ideology at all by whether he drinks his tea with a spoon in his glass.

Another thing that obviously would not go out with the war was the new attitude toward religion. More people were going to services now than at any time since the revolution. Plans were being made for extensive repair and reconstruction of churches. I learned that even some Komsomols, who used to spend lots of time denouncing priests, now insisted that a church wedding was the only fitting way to solemnize what, under new laws, becomes virtually an indissoluble pact. But I shall have more to say about the new place of religion in Russia in a later chapter.

IV

Marriage and Motherhood

You could hear almost as many opinions on the new maternity and divorce laws, decreed in July, as you heard elsewhere on the Polish-border question, and colored by just as many arguments, pro and con. And to the Soviet citizen the future of his married life seemed more important than the future of Lvov—even though he could pronounce "Lvov" a lot easier than we can.

No one objected to the generous additional state provisions for mothers and their children, but the same ukase which promised them to Russians was linked with stringent new regulations concerning the dissolution of wedlock. Thousands of divorces formerly were given to dissatisfied spouses when they merely signed post cards making the request to the marriage bureau, but the new law drastically changed all that. According to its own preamble, the edict of July, 1944, was a further step toward "consolidation of the Soviet family." The Moscow press even referred to it as the "charter of the Soviet family." It was asserted to be the logical consequence of experiment and experience over a period of twenty-five years. Yet some foreign critics maintained that the whole thing was simply "another reversion to capitalist practice" and "another move toward social conservatism." What was the truth?

On the face of it, the new statute did seem to resemble our own more closely than before. The law provided for increased solemnity in the ceremony itself, and the church is a good place for that. Other aspects of the law must have been noted with favor in the Vatican. But there were also innovations which shocked the clergy more than ever, and made the Red family like no other.

The basic thing is the key relationship adopted by the state toward the mother and her offspring. The Soviet Government now assumes such broad responsibilities, quite independent of the male in the case, that fatherhood's age-old duties of breadwinner and protector of the brood seem largely usurped. At first glance, too, the male appears to be liberated. He can no longer be named in court as the father of a child of an unmarried mother. He can no longer be sued for alimony.

"But it only looks easy to us," a Russian of the presumably emancipated sex assured me. "If you examine the law closely you see that a man's apparent freedom of action in one respect is more than counterbalanced by strict responsibility for his oath of matrimony." The male may enjoy his extra-marital fling, but a legal change of spouses is another matter. The No. 1 wife can now feel very secure indeed, especially if she is a mother.

Again, the woman who wants children without being encumbered by a male dropping cigarette ashes around and entertaining undesirable friends, can legally have them, and the state accords her honors and upkeep. She has more freedom than before because she has more security. Theoretically, the institution of old maids might go out with the same broom that sweeps away divorce. Yet unmarried motherhood holds no more attraction for Russians than it does for any other women.

Then why the law? The answer has to be sought elsewhere, in the state's primary concern for the Soviet child of whatever origin. Profound interest in the birthright and welfare of Ivan, Jr., was in fact held to justify the entire ukase.

Formerly Soviet law supported the view that "marriage and divorce are private and personal affairs," although whenever children were involved the state had a right to intervene. In now establishing all marriages as "matters of public interest and concern," the new law greatly emphasizes Soviet paternalism toward the child. The Government which promulgated the edict begins to look rather like the benevolent patriarch who, doting on progeny, leaves his sons and daughters a bounty which they can inherit only after producing a certain number of grandchildren, and offers them additional inducements providing the fullest opportunity for a healthy and equally privileged childhood for all his descendants, however numerous.

Childbearing was subsidized in the Soviet Union even before the war. The state granted a sum of nine dollars* for the baby's layette and a food allowance of from one to two dollars a month during the infant's first year. With an average birth rate of some 6,000,000 a year, those items alone were estimated to cost the state more than $160,000,000. In addition, the mother of more than six children was entitled to a bonus of $400 annually for five years, and to a further bonus of $1000 for each subsequent birth. Hundreds of thousands of Soviet families collected payment on such claims.

The old law also guaranteed working women nine weeks of prenatal leave with pay. This cost the Soviet bursars somewhere in the vicinity of a billion dollars annually. If such earlier com-

* Figured at official exchange rate, Rs.5 =$1.

pensations were intended to reconcile women to the law which forbids abortion (except for medical reasons), then the present improved version of benefits may help somewhat to win approval for the tightening-up against divorce. Anyway, it was interesting to see in this instance, as in others, a highly practical demonstration of the Soviet theory that law is an instrument for achievement of constructive social ends, and can be effective only when its purely repressive aspects are counter-pointed by positive inducements to compliance.

Marriage in Russia isn't merely an institution; it is now a partnership that pays dividends that increase with the progeny. Monetary awards for motherhood begin today with the birth of the third child, when the state makes a gift of eighty dollars in cash. This is in addition to the layette fee, raised to twenty-four dollars. With the birth of a fourth child, by a mother of three living children, the state makes a down payment of $260, and beginning with the second year of the baby's life, the mother receives a monthly subsidy of sixteen dollars—for four years. From then on the gains mount on the following scale:

> With the arrival of the fifth child, cash payment $340, monthly allowance $24; sixth child, payment $400, monthly allowance $28; seventh child, payment $500, allowance $40; eighth, payment $500, allowance $40; ninth, payment $700, allowance $50; tenth, payment $700, allowance $50. Thereafter $1000 for each future president, and $60 monthly allowance.

The triumph of ten births is further accorded prestige by the bestowal on the author of the Order of Mother Heroine, with an appropriate decoration. The Glory of Motherhood medal, in several classes, is given for lesser attainments. And a number of additional economic and social advantages are guaranteed to prospective mothers which, while the war lasted, meant more than the actual cash benefits.

Pregnancy leave with pay is extended to seventy-seven days, and expectant mothers are excused from overtime work four months after childbirth. Food rations are doubled during pregnancy, and additional food and clothing become available. New rest homes and milk kitchens and medical and child centers were opened. It became compulsory for all factories and institutions employing women to maintain nurseries, kindergartens and mother-and-child rooms.

Unmarried mothers seem to be somewhat better compensated than married ones, for obvious reasons. State aid for them begins with the first child, at twenty dollars monthly, rises to thirty dollars for two children, and forty dollars for three children. Thereafter, unmarried mothers also receive the full bonuses, allowances and honors accorded to the wedded. The unmarried mother is entitled to state aid until her child is twelve, whereas in the case of married mothers state aid stops when the child is five. The state also maintains "homes for little children," where unmarried mothers may install their infants for any period up to twelve years, free of charge.

Tsarist law denied legal status to both unmarried mothers and their offspring, but under Soviet law all children have always been regarded as legitimate. The July edict did not change that, and the unmarried mother can still give her child any surname she chooses. In the early days, Communists often were quite casual about marriage. Frequently mothers kept their own names and sometimes they bestowed them on their children. But after July, tens of thousands of Russian couples who never bothered to register as man and wife hastened to solemnize and legalize both marriage and offspring—sometimes with a church ceremony. The new law gives common-law mothers no right to claim husbands' estates and other benefits.

There are many cases in which the Soviet father may be married to a woman other than the mother of his children. Formerly, no social odium was inferred for the position of such unmarried mothers, as their children were considered legitimate. Their status now becomes somewhat ambiguous, but the new law gives them the promise of state support, as to an unmarried woman with a child. Obviously, that measure is to some extent

dictated by war problems created in areas formerly occupied by
the Germans, where there are thousands of fatherless children.

As in Britain, and to some extent in America, many births
have resulted from "war romances" where there was no marriage. In some cases, the fathers of such children have been
killed; in others, the fathers were already married to somebody
else. The fact that new homes to receive infants of unmarried
mothers were opened as far away as Novosibirsk suggested that
this problem was not confined to war areas in Russia.

In a country where state planning and "socialist emulation" are
accepted features of society, in a country where labor is compensated on a piece-work basis with what are claimed to be satisfactory results, the new system of honors and rewards for
motherhood seemed destined to bring about the desired "consolidation of the family."

The divorce law is in itself part of the new plan to inspire
motherhood. Here, as elsewhere, a certain percentage of
couples had entered matrimony with a somewhat tentative attitude, avoiding children in order to be free to disentangle themselves if the marriage failed. Now unsure spouses find themselves with narrowed opportunities for second thoughts. The
new law may make marriage for better or for worse, but anyway
it seems to make it virtually for keeps.

Until July, 1944, you could legally "write yourself out" of
marriage about as easily as you could "write yourself in." In
practice, however, divorce had for some time been severely
deprecated among party members and Komsomols. It was almost as much a black mark on a party record as was sexual
promiscuity. The revolutionary period of loose living in Russia
was actually very brief, and Lenin himself led those who denounced "free love." During the past decade Communists assumed what some consider a puritanical attitude toward sex
relations, and the new law directly reflects it.

No one can now regain his freedom except after airing his
marital troubles in public. The steps are many, difficult and ex-

pensive. First, a petition to the People's Court, accompanied by Rs.200. At the same time, an advertisement in the papers. Not till the advertisement has been printed—and so far each paper has limited its columns to two announcements per week—can the Court act. Then the answering of summonses to explain the case, the rounding up of witnesses, and attempts by the Court to dissuade the couple. In the event of failure to reconcile, the case may be referred to a higher Court. And if, finally, the divorce is granted, the plaintiff has to pay a fee of from $100 to $2,000. Very few would-be divorcees are persistent enough to go through such a rigmarole.

"The worst feature of all," according to an acquaintance of mine who was contemplating divorce before the law changed, "is the advertisement in the press. In Russian eyes, it seems a form of public disgrace. It is like a political self-denunciation. People will put up with almost anything rather than do that."

Do the Soviet fathers really think they can abolish divorce? Probably not. Yet a few years ago, when there were 52,000 legal abortions in Moscow in one year alone, it was considered preposterous that abortion could be prohibited. Nevertheless, against much more vocal opposition than one heard against the "anti-divorce" law, the prohibition of abortion was enforced and today the exceptions are few. It remains to be seen whether people can be talked out of divorce to the same extent. One thing is certain: if the law doesn't accomplish its purpose the Soviet rulers will not hesitate to throw it away and try something else. Russia wants the biggest birth-rate in the world to fill up all those empty places left by the war.

Marxism Vindicated?

FEW onlookers in Moscow were yet willing to predict just what kind of society would emerge from the poundings of the war, and most Russians sensed that many unknown adjustments lay ahead. Trying to know what was going on and what would happen after the war was like listening in on a telephone when the operator leaves the switch open at a central exchange. We can hear many voices, but they are all just outside our focus of sound.

This much was certain, even to a newly returned correspondent. Nothing had been done or said which suggested any intention of abandoning the main body of Marxist-Leninist teachings as the foundation of the state. Much had recently happened to indicate that the study of historical materialism would be emphasized in future training, even more than in the past.

While a large percentage of party members were fighting in the Army there had been some relaxation in the strict regime of Marxist study, in favor of the practical art of warfare. Discussions were in many instances reduced to the party secretary lecturing members in the form of "highly one-sided reports," the press announced. Now it was stressed by such party organs as *Agitator, Propagandist,* and *Bolshevik* that the "forgotten" party statute instructing secretaries to arrange political debates and conferences, as well as to promote self-study and self-education in Marxism among the workers, must be strictly enforced. "Upon the thorough Marxist education of party members and the entire Soviet intelligentsia depends not only the successful outcome of the war but likewise the solution of all subsequent problems."

Odd conclusions were drawn by some writers in America, after a dissertation published in *Under the Banner of Marxism*, which was a commentary on the new official *Short History of the Soviet Union* issued last year. I carefully read the 10,000-word document in Moscow. Clearly it was written to establish the fact that the law of value still operates under Soviet socialism, as distinct from the former rather vague theory of an idyllic communism in which that law might lose its meaning. Put in layman's terms, the whole essay was in effect merely a long-winded justification of the piece-work system of payment and differentiation in wage scales as practiced in the USSR—which were already clearly provided for in the Constitution of 1936.

Yet some American critics had decided that the article amounted to an admission that the laws of capitalist economy were now admitted to apply in Russia. They simply ignored the main argument of *Under the Banner of Marxism*. They ignored also its reaffirmations of superiorities of Marxist-Leninist-Stalinist teachings and practices over those of all capitalist economists, and its reiterations of some fundamental irreconcilabilities. They ignored statements like this: "Socialism is the highest stage of development of society compared to all preceding systems of production." And, "Socialism assures tempos of development greater than in principal capitalist countries."

No, this country does not intend to let go of its system. New histories will interpret Russian victory as the complete vindication of all past socialist study and planning, and will identify it spiritually and organically with Communist Party leadership. At the same time Soviet leaders were fully aware of the great role in salvation of the Soviet Union played by the help of capitalist countries, especially the United States, in supplying vital equipment and food which the Soviet system was unable to produce. They likewise realized that further help would be needed for a long time in overcoming obstacles lying ahead. Despite her enormous military prestige, Russia would not promote proletarian revolutions in Europe where it meant jeopardizing continued co-operation with the United States.

The Russian people are tired of war and they do not want a policy likely to cause serious conflict with nations whose friendship they need while convalescent. They want peace and a chance to build up their own country, whose grandeur they realize more fully than ever before. War has taught them that anything is possible for this country, if they work for it.

"I sometimes think it was almost worth going through all this," one man said to me, "just for us to learn how to work. We have millions of skilled people now who knew nothing about machinery before and would probably never have learned except for the war. We know how to use machines more efficiently now and our leaders have learned how to organize industry to get the most out of it. Of course we are still far from your American standards—but we've got the rhythm of it at last, we have hit our stride, we've discovered what we can really do. We have the people in the factories in the East we needed there so long— and we have some of them working there *willingly* for the first time. The working man now believes in his ability to master his job and any machine you can make. We've learned how to work at last."

One day I walked back from Spasso House, after dining with our Ambassador, Averell Harriman, with Anatole Litvak, the Hollywood director who made *The Battle for Russia* and was now a lieutenant colonel in the American Army Signal Corps. Litvak was back in Moscow, where his mother still lived, for the first time in twenty years. I asked him what changes he noticed.

"The city is still recognizable," he replied, "but I wouldn't have known the people. They aren't the same Russians. They are sad, but proud and confident and full of hope—even my old mother. The Russia I remember was humble and pessimistic and defeated before it began. I have talked to many Russians now. They say something like this, 'I've lost my son,' or 'I've lost my brother,' or 'I've lost my husband.' 'The roof leaks and I have paper soles in my shoes.' Then they look at the rockets celebrating victory and they say, 'But the worst is over. Tomorrow's another day.'"

But what would that tomorrow bring for Europe, which Hitler's approaching collapse and Russian victory were confronting with a choice unprecedented in history? Some of the answers will, I hope, be found all through the latter chapters of this book —and toward the end I shall attempt to summarize the meaning of the many new features that Soviet society has taken on during the war. And here a good beginning toward understanding Russia's role in a world freed of Hitlerism can be made in Rumania, the first Axis satellite to fall to the banners of Marshal Stalin's Red Army.

CHAPTER TWO

Stalin Enters the Balkans

I

Peace—But Not Communism

IN THE early summer some of us flew down to Bessarabia, by then re-incorporated into the Soviet Union, and went by car across the Prut River into Rumania, where for the first time the Red Army broke onto the native soil of an Axis enemy. Here in the historic corridor leading down to the mouth of the Danube and to the soft sparkle of the Black Sea the crude outline of a new pattern of life was beginning to form, a pattern that would eventually spill across the frontiers of all the Danubian countries. Soon the Red Army would cross into Transylvania and join hands with the fighting partisans of Marshal Tito. Soon it would enter the mountain passes that gird Bulgaria, to cut off the road to Greece and reach into Belgrade, to block the Nazis' retreat from Siberia. Soon it would storm the gates of Budapest, and finally descend upon Hitler's native Austria.

What use would the Soviet Government make of its victory in the first of these Balkan lands to fall to the Red banner—the homeland of King Carol, who had led his people into catastrophe and the ruling class itself toward suicide? Was Russia interested in rewards beyond seeing its Rumanian enemies crushed and made to pay heavy reparations? How would Stalin exact retribution for crimes which included the murder of some 200,000 Soviet citizens in Odessa alone—according to official Soviet claims? Would the Kremlin control the political, social and cultural life of Rumania? If not, what kind of state would emerge to succeed the doomed dictatorship of General Ion Antonescu, to whom Carol had surrendered the fate of the nation?

We knew that Russia had subscribed to the terms of the Atlantic Charter and to the phrases of the Moscow and Teheran declarations, which promise the future security of all nations, including sovereign life even to Axis satellites. We knew that Premier Molotov had made a specific announcement, when the Red Army entered Rumania, guaranteeing to respect its territorial frontiers and not to interfere with Rumanian institutions. How well was the Red Army observing these self-imposed obligations? How would it behave in the future?

The truth is that those questions, which mean so much not simply to the Balkans but to all members of that "world family of democratic nations" discussed at the Teheran conference, cannot be answered fully for perhaps a decade. But I can tell you something about what it was like when the Red Army conquered Rumania and from this you may be able to piece together the pattern of a destiny soon to unfold throughout the Balkans.

In Dorohoi and Botosani, two prefectures in Rumanian Moldavia which had been held by the Russians since April, 1944, I talked to mayors and to village officials, to trade unionists and to farms, to Jewish refugees from Antonescu's concentration camps and to a Rumanian chief of police, to representatives of several large American business organizations and to a mother superior in a Rumanian convent.

All these people, some with satisfaction and others with regret, agreed on one thing: they said the Russians had not instigated any revolutionary movements. They said the Red Army had observed the Molotov declaration with disciplined correctness—and we saw the declaration posted wherever the hammer and sickle flew.

There appeared to be no open effort by the Red Army to propagandize the masses in favor of communism or socialism. Pictures of the King and Queen and of the late Dowager Queen Marie still hung on the walls of official buildings, while Stalin's portrait was strangely absent, except in offices of the Red Army. On the surface of things, nothing suggested that the inhabitants did not enjoy a degree of liberty which, considering that Rumania was still a country at war against Russia, was astonishing. In fact, many of the Rumanians apparently wanted to fight on the winning side now. The handsome young Russian commandant of Dorohoi told me that peasants were coming to him every day, asking to enlist in the Red Army.

"The loyalty of the population is remarkable," said he. "Men wish to become soldiers and women wish to join up as nurses. We have to refuse as politely as we can."

Elsewhere, I was told by Vian Bogsan, a former chief of police who had resigned his commission in the Rumanian Army before the Reds arrived, that he could easily recruit a pro-Allied army. He said he would gladly offer his services if the Allies would furnish arms. But while the Russians used the local population for labor when necessary, they evidently considered the peasants unsuitable for a volunteer army.

Meanwhile, no drastic changes had as yet been effected in Rumanian laws, customs or institutions. The Antonescu ban on political parties had not been officially lifted; property laws remained unchanged; private trade continued as before. The same forms of government, and even some of the same personnel, still prevailed.

All in all, the Prisoner of Zenda still seemed a credible story in the atmosphere preserved here. The peasants had not yet put on shoes, nor forgotten to take off their caps before gentlemen—and judging from demonstrations a gentleman meant everybody who wore shoes and wasn't a Jew. And if you asked the Rumanians whom they wanted to govern them after the war, and whether they wanted the monarchy or a republic, likely as not they would answer, "Why, King Carol, of course! This fellow Antonescu has stirred up too much trouble for us, and King Michael is too young to handle him."

Communism? The peasants said they didn't know what it was.

The king and dynasty—they were something everybody understood. But they all knew one thing: they wanted peace. "If we
could have peace"—an old peasant woman broke in when her
husband was explaining to me why he was a "liberal," and for
King Carol—"if we could have peace, we would even put up
with a republic."

II

Improbable Appearances

AND yet the external wounds of war hereabouts seemed re-
markably few compared with any combat area I had seen in
Russia, and it was hard to believe the Red Army would, indefinitely, refuse to help itself to booty to recoup Soviet losses. The
whole region of Botosani was taken without fighting, in the Russian grand encirclement. I heard details about this from Evelyn
May Tormry, a white-haired Irish lady from Dublin who had
lived in Botosani for thirty years, but still had a brogue that
would span the Danube.

"We just woke up one morning and there, without a sound,
were the Russians," she told me. "They had come in during the
night and not one person was killed."

But nothing seemed quite real in this country—including Mrs.
Tormry. It was tragic, pathetic, comic, and you had to keep rub-
bing your eyes to believe in its *opera-bouffe* effect. The warm
welcome these people gave you, their nominal foe; the brazen
or stupid contempt with which Rumanian officials spoke of their
peasantry before listening Red Army officers who were themselves the sons of peasants; the rough but richly embroidered

garb of the country folk, who stood gaping at you across picket
fences over which spilled roses and grapes; the romantic beauty
of the purple hills carpeted with tawny wheat fields bordered
with wild flowers; the quaint cobbled streets of the towns and
the broken-down carriages drawn between lines of undersized
houses; the nuns chanting prayers in rooms heavy with incense,
while Red Army officers stood with lowered heads and tongues
in cheeks: it all added up to a fantasy conceived in Hollywood
and lacking only usherettes and bingo to complete the illusion.

This state of improbability was further heightened by incidents like these. You were entertained by local talent in Botosani, where a Jewish member of the "Jaszboy Band" sang for you
—in an English version translated from the Rumanian—"My
Heart Belongs to Daddy." Only, instead of daddy, he sang of a
heart that belonged "to my very nice girl." You went to a banquet and even the local rum and brandy seemed bogus. You
were honored by another local orchestra playing favorite airs
of the Red Army, but when it stood up to render "the American
national anthem," it turned out to be Yankee Doodle.

Things did not seem to clarify much more when you investi-
gated more closely. Why was the Irish lady, Evelyn Tormry,who
had never acknowledged the Free State of Eire and who still
held an English passport, never interned by the Rumanians?
Why? Because the Rumanians had really loved the British all
along. So they told us. At a tea given in our honor the beavered
mayor of Dorohoi devoted ninety percent of his speech to fondly
recalling the historic ties of friendship between his country in
general, and himself in particular, for dear old Britannia.

"Rumanian freedom," he declaimed, "was born in England.
For 400 years English blood has been shed for Rumanian freedom! You have given us Queen Marie! Every Rumanian reveres
Queen Marie as a second mother. She had English blood, but the
soul of a Rumanian!" Choking voice, tear-dimmed eyes; it was
wonderful.

Surely Rumania's ancient friends, the English, could under-

stand Mayor Lovenescu's feelings? Surely the Americans, "who
are fighting for the freedom of small nations" (against the Bolsheviks, like us, he seemed to hint), would also understand that
the dynasty really meant no harm to its old allies? Surely a way
would be found to save Rumania from the consequences of the
mistakes of her rulers, the slight error of shooting a few hundred
thousand Russians? Red Army officers listened to all this with
bulging eyes and shut lips.

"They've been well trained, these Red Army men," remarked
a colleague. "Did you ever see such discipline?"

But we had few doubts about the political future of M.
Lovenescu.

One thing was clear. The Soviet Government, if it had any
plan for this country, was in no haste to reveal it. The evidence
suggested that the Russians expected Rumania's internal questions would solve themselves, in the later stages of the war itself.
Already, without direct intervention of the Red Army to bring
about specific reforms, the basis of the old order was collapsing
under the weight of the miscalculations of its own leaders. The
occupation simply created the conditions in which a new kind
of Rumanian leadership could find birth.

III

Decay and Vitality

THE former rulers, the fascists and their sympathizers, were
already in flight and some had reached Bulgaria and Turkey.
Their evacuation from Dorohoi and Botosani had been arranged
by the Government and paid for in advance of the arrival of the

Russians. Only a handful of landlords and capitalists, those few who had retired from political life after the advent of Antonescu, had dared stay behind. Since many of the former officials and army officers were closely identified with large property owners, their disappearance naturally meant new adjustments in ownership and management. For the present their shops and factories had been taken over by the prefectural government, which had rented them, in some cases, to committees of workmen.

Trade unions had sprung back into life. Ninety percent of the workers of Botosani were members of one of the seven unions that had quickly reasserted themselves. The bakers' union had compelled employers to abolish night work, to increase wages by fifty percent, and to provide a daily bread ration of 600 grams for each worker. What was perhaps more interesting, they had insisted that, in order to reduce costs, and so to make bread available for all, only one standard brand should be baked. They had won their point—with the Red Army backing them.

Here the unions had their own football teams, their choirs, and an orchestra and library. There had been labor unions in the past, of course, but Antonescu had suppressed them in totalitarian manner, and interned their leaders. Union committeemen said that many of their former leaders were taken from prison and burned to death by the Germans in the notorious Rebiatsu camp.

"Even before Antonescu came to power, the merchants and factory owners were always able to bribe the police to suppress us," according to Jacob Tippol, the Rumanian chairman of the trade unions association. "Now they can no longer do so. In the old days, the authorities took no interest in us, and the Army was always on the side of employers against labor."

Nothing was accomplished in Antonescu's Rumania without bribery, it seemed, and it was customary to pay the police to arrest your personal enemy. But you had to be sure your bribe was bigger than the other fellow's; otherwise he would outbid you and you would find yourself in jail. One man told of a case when thirty police officers were sent out to arrest thirty criminals, all known to be in town. Nineteen came back without their men, but presumably not empty-handed. A second batch was sent out and seven came back alone. It took four trips and four sets of policemen to bring in all the culprits.

Under the Red Army labor was no longer persecuted by the police, and local leaders asserted that the Russians did not interfere in employer-employee disputes, "except that the Red Army is not used against labor." (A very big exception!) Union men disclaimed membership in the Communist Party. I asked whether there were Communist sympathizers among them and their spokesman finally replied, "Remember, we are workers!"

Surreptitiously, when we were in public places here and there, at luncheons or teas, or meeting the Chamber of Commerce, local people came up to tell us what was, or what they thought was, going on behind the scenes. Everybody seemed to speak English. One local merchant, who had been to America, told me the Russians had already organized two anti-Hitler Rumanian divisions, from among war prisoners. He also pointed out the leader of the local Communist Party, which he said was actively organizing labor, with the consent of the Russians.

Another time a rather pretty Jewish girl introduced herself, speaking excellent English, to ask whether I had any recent copies of *Time* or the *Saturday Evening Post,* which she used to read regularly. All she wanted was to get out of Rumania— and she wanted me to get her a visa. "We are not poor, we are rich," she emphasized. I had to explain that the State Department couldn't be bribed.

The prefectural governments also had the responsibility now for controlling the estates of absentee or *émigré* landlords, and this situation was handled like the problem presented by abandoned factories. Such estates were expropriated, in much the same manner as the guerrillas in North China utilized land belonging to owners who had sought shelter in Japanese-held cities. One nettling problem was what to do with Jewish pro-

prietors who came back after the arrival of the Russians, to re-
claim the lands which Antonescu had taken from them.

"About 150 estates in this prefecture were formerly owned by
Jews," explained Col. Vladimir Chernizhev, the twenty-five-year-
old commandant at Botosani. "Many of the landlords were unpopular with the peasants. It was decided not to return these
estates to their former owners, since the law of the country pro-
hibits it, anyway. The Red Army can't change the law; it will
have to wait till there's a new government in Bucharest. In the
meantime the land is being tilled by the peasants as a commune,
and they pay the state half of their crop as rent."

Another surprise for the peasants was an astounding reduction
in taxes. In Brauscauti village, near Dorohoi, the village chief,
Alexei Georgi, told me that whereas farmers with ten hectares
used to pay annual taxes of 1,000 Rumanian lei, or about ten
American dollars, they now paid only 200 lei.

"There was a lot of surtaxes, which have also been abolished," said Georgi. "Things are better now, you see; we pay
less taxes."

War taxes had been abolished for city dwellers too. But in
both the city and village the prefectural government, not the
Russians, was given credit for this phenomenon.

"You are too poor to pay now," Georgi reported that the pre-
fect had explained to him, "but after the war, your taxes will
increase again." So Georgi was keeping his fingers crossed.

I talked with many Rumanian Jews. You couldn't have avoided
talking to them, if you had wanted to; they followed you down
the streets with their fears, complaints and addresses of relatives
in America. All of them seemed to be building their own hopes
for the future on Anglo-American understanding of their problems. They were surprised and disappointed when told that
there was no likelihood of American troops occupying Rumania.
They admitted that they were no longer persecuted; they no
longer liver in terror; they breathed as free men and women;
they were not starving. But still—"When will the Allies occupy

Rumania and make it possible for Jews to emigrate to Britain and America?"

Russians said they could not understand it. Why should these people want to leave their native land? *Their* land? Even the anti-Jewish laws still remained on the statute books, though in practice they were no longer completely observed. No wonder Jews were anxious about the future! How could they ever feel secure in Rumania again?

There was something inexpressibly sad about the Rumanians here and you felt the poignance of it especially when you saw them in the mass, measured against the big, proud peasants of the Red Army. On the streets of the towns traffic was directed by tough, melon-breasted imported Russian girls—perhaps specially selected to impress the undersized Rumanians and Jews, who regarded them with awe and astonishment. These women seemed to symbolize for the local inhabitants all that propaganda had taught them was most awesome and fearful about Slavic Bolshevism.

I remember how it was at a joint concert put on for our benefit, where pathetic dancing and singing by the local Jews, and especially their attempts to sing Rumanian folk songs (of a culture which had denied them any role), strangely contrasted with the storm of exuberant power, perfect co-ordination and magnificent voices of the Red Army performers and chorus on the same stage. On the one hand, a melancholy, leaderless, benighted people, whether Jews or Rumanians; on the other, bright-eyed, educated, emancipated Red peasants, sure of themselves and full of eager confidence for the future.

> *Our mothers are our cannon,*
> *Our sisters are our swords,*
> *Our wives are our well-loaded rifles,*
> *Our grandfathers are our victories!*

It was an old Russian battle song composed by men of Kutuzov's army when they met Napoleon at Borodino, and now it was back in favor again, along with Kutuzov and Suvorov. Rich young voices lifted it to the roof and the audience of local people seemed filled at once with admiration and trepidation before such vitality. At that moment you could not but feel that, however it may have been in the past, every Russian would in the future worship Stalin as the man who led Russia to the greatest military glory in its history.

IV

Rumanian Destiny

AT FIRST you wondered how it was that so many Jews were left alive, but inquiry soon revealed that bribery and corruption and the deviousness of administration had extended even to the enforcement of Antonescu's anti-Semitic laws. The Jews paid millions of dollars in ransom money. In Botosani alone, in 1941, Antonescu's agents extracted $600,000 from them for the Rumanian war chest and for their own pockets. The "contribution" was forthcoming after a trainload of Jews in neighboring Dorohoi, who had refused to fork over, were shipped to a concentration camp where half of them subsequently died of starvation. In 1942, the Jews of Botosani paid again—four times the 1941 figure. In 1943, Antonescu squeezed $40,000,000 from the Jews of all Rumania.

How was it that so many Jews here still owned their shops and houses, after the anti-Semitic decrees? The Antonescu Government had confiscated all Jewish property and offered it for sale to non-Jewish Rumanians. But in practice many of the Rumanian purchasers borrowed their money from the original Jewish owners, who continued to maintain occupation while paying "dividends" to their phony Rumanian partners. So if you were a Jew with money, you kept your freedom and even your property. But when you became a Jew without money, you went to a concentration camp or into a labor battalion. But not into the army.

"We Jews were not allowed to become soldiers," complained one ragged subject, recently demobilized from a labor battalion. "The Rumanians said we wouldn't fight."

The hands-off policy of the Red Army extended to all religious groups. At a Rumanian convent I noticed that the sisters had not thought it necessary even to remove from their walls a curious religious map, which showed the sphere of influence of the Rumanian church and state extending far into Russia as well as throughout the Balkans. Priests of the Old Believers, an orthodox sect of the former Russian state religion, told me they were fully satisfied with the treatment they were getting. They were even planning to send an investigating commission to Russia to see whether conditions were favorable for their return to the homeland. These Old Believers had left Russia two centuries ago, after a dispute with the church authorities of that period. At the invitation of Tsar Nicholas I, the sect once sent a mission to Russia before the last war. But they hadn't liked the looks of things and so had stayed on here in Northern Rumania.

Summing up, it seemed that life was no worse in Rumania for those who had stayed behind to greet the Russians, and that there were definite improvements for most people. The conservative peasant still had his land and kept more of the product of his labor. There were still plenty of cattle about. The worker had freedom and a sense of new power. The Jew was out of the concentration camps. He had equal rights and a chance to live. All had religious freedom; churches and their institutions were not being molested.

There were plenty of indications, however, that the Russians would not tolerate a recrudescence of that kind of leadership which had driven Rumania into an alliance with Hitler. Elements in the population who supported Antonescu's short-lived Rumanian rhapsody, the dream of greater empire built upon a Transnistria carved out of Russia, would also disappear from the political map of the Balkans.

I ended a dispatch to the *Saturday Evening Post* about Red occupation of Rumania with the following paragraphs:

"What, then, will be left to organize a new Rumanian society? Obviously the backbone of the old state will remain the backbone of the new: the hat-in-hand, meekly bowing peasantry. But now it may stiffen with a long-delayed realization that it has vertebrate possibilities of its own. After the fall of Bucharest the workers also will emerge, as in Botosani, from the recesses into which fascism has driven them, emerge timidly at first, and then with rising consciousness of power.

"From the concentration camps will come some survivors of pre-fascism, the intellectuals, the anti-Hitler political leaders. They, and the suppressed Peasant, Liberal and Communist Parties, may together furnish a leadership that can make free and upright men from this dark serf-like material spread across these troubled mountains.

"*Whatever it is called, that new regime, like all regimes to come in this part of the world, inevitably will have to lean heavily on the friendship and understanding of the giant to the east. First of all because it is to Russia that they will be most heavily indebted for reparations, and the way those payments are exacted can determine the fate of any future order in the Danubian countries. Secondly, and more fundamentally, because the Soviet Union, with its boundless energy and vitality, can no longer be excluded as a formative influence in the entire Balkan world.*"

The Soviet censor passed all of it, rather to my surprise. If I could have written perfectly frankly I would have altered nothing except the word "formative," in the last sentence. "Major external influence" would have been a more exact description.

And a few weeks later, when I met the Rumanian Communist Party chieftain, Lucretiu Patrascanu, in Moscow, where he was

sent by King Michael to negotiate an armistice for a new Rumanian regime, after the success of the Soviet offensive in Moldavia, everything he said seemed to me to confirm that earlier
judgment.

V

Patrascanu & Co.

LUCRETIU PATRASCANU made a good impression on all of us who
saw him after he came above ground in Moscow. He was a dark
and rather handsome Rumanian lawyer, forty-two years old,
who had served six terms in jail. He had, in fact, been in a concentration camp when the Russians invaded Rumania. King
Michael secretly secured his release, and had him brought to the
palace. There he conferred with leaders of the Labor and Liberal
Parties, to advise the King and his Regent what course was left
open for the country. Patrascanu was authorized to contact the
Russians, in the King's name.

At that time, or perhaps even earlier, Moscow told the Rumanians that a speedy withdrawal from the war, and some help
in throwing the Germans out of the Danube valley, would be re-
warded by Soviet support for Rumania's ancient claims to Transylvania, against Hungary. Apparently other Rumanian delegates, who were secretly meeting Allied diplomats in Cairo,
were given the same assurances. Anyway it was largely that
promise which decided the King to cast his lot with the Red
Army and get rid of an unwelcome alliance with Hitler. In May
he recognized the National Democratic Bloc, which was secretly
formed among the Communists, Social Democrats, Peasant

Party and Patriotic Union, to prepare for a *coup d'Etat* against
Antonescu's Government.

However, the Red Army was unable to renew its major drive
in the Balkans till late in the summer, at the conclusion of the
Soviet offensive in the Baltic states and Eastern Poland. When
Marshal Malinovsky's Ukrainian troops began to drive down
the Danube again, the Germans still had 660,000 troops in Rumania, but most of them were at the front. Patrascanu asked the
King to increase his forces in the capital and August 26th was
fixed as the date for an uprising. Antonescu got wind of it and
three days in advance went to see the King to demand sweeping
new powers. Michael acted very decisively, however; instead of
submitting he ordered the Palace Guards to arrest Antonescu
and members of his Cabinet.

Raging, the German commandant paid a visit to the King at
two A.M., to demand a renewal of the pledge of alliance with
Hitler. The King declined. Two hours later fighting began in the
streets of Bucharest—and four days later, to everybody's astonishment including the Rumanians', the Germans withdrew in
defeat. Whatever you could say about the poor performance of
Rumanian troops up to that moment, it had to be admitted that
the behavior of the insurrectionists in Bucharest—in which thousands of half-trained workers took part—was brilliantly successful. It saved many Russian lives. A masterpiece of planning, it
was the result of full liaison which anti-Hitlerite Rumanians established four months in advance with the Red Army. It offered
a glaring contrast with the disastrous uprising in Warsaw led by
the anti-Soviet General Bor, who had no previous understanding
with the Red Army whatsoever. From the time of the Bucharest
coup onward the whole German position in the Balkans was
doomed. Before the year was out the doughty little Ukrainian
Marshal, Rodion Malinovsky, who had been chasing the Nazis
ever since Stalingrad, would enter Belgrade and shake hands
with Marshal Tito.

Patrascanu accepted the armistice in the name of the King,

and under the circumstances the terms seemed surprisingly moderate. Rumania had to pay an indemnity of 300 million dollars, no more than that imposed on Finland. She lost no territory and earned a chance, by joining in an alliance with Russia, of getting back her pre-war control of Transylvania, which Hitler had handed over to Hungary's Admiral Horthy. Patrascanu seemed to think he had made a fair bargain.

One afternoon a group of us had tea with Patrascanu's chic, vivacious and smartly dressed French-speaking wife, who didn't look any more like the highly sophisticated Communist (which she was) than Gloria Vanderbilt, ex Cicco.

"How long will King Michael last in the new Rumania?" someone asked her.

"Perhaps two years," she suggested.

"And how long will it be before the Communists—Rumanians, of course—are running the country?"

"Two years," she said very sweetly.

CHAPTER THREE

Polish Interlude

I

Preface for Skeptics

ORDINARILY, a writer ought to eschew subjects already fully reported in the daily press. But once in a while you run across a story so sublime in its witness to the divinity of man, or so loathsome as to make the meanest beast seem clean and wholesome by comparison, that it renews itself through the continued interest or incredulity of the public, and through the subjective experience of the reporter.

Maidanek was such a story, in the second category. For Poland and Russia, at least, Maidanek and the ghosts that throng around it would be a living presence at the peace tables to harden man's heart to the inevitable dismemberment of Germany. Quite apart from its scientific interest, it is important for Americans to remember it, and in all conscience I cannot shirk my part in contributing to the record of it. Russians will never forget it. To them it is one of the gravest of many scores to settle.

When the history of this war is written, Maidanek may best epitomize the inner nature of Nazi philosophy and mark its most brilliant success in perverting the very virtues of a once-great people into the service of a machinery of crime almost too monstrous for the human mind to accept. Even after seeing the abundant evidence, hearing the statements of eye-witnesses and listening to the confessions of a few of the murderers themselves, there is a voice in man taught to revere human life as sacred that continues to say all this could not happen. Yet when I look

43

at my notes, taken at Lublin, during a trip to liberated Poland, when I review the accumulation of testimony, intelligence informs me, as it does every other observer I know who has had this unenviable opportunity, that the main story of this death factory, to which the Nazis themselves unofficially referred as the Camp for Extermination, has been truthfully reported.

How many people were destroyed at Maidanek? I have no way of knowing precisely. Two Germans who worked in the camp told us that on a single day, November 3rd of 1943, between 17,000 and 20,000 men, women and children were obliterated there. They agreed also that "hundreds" at a time had been taken out of the gas chambers on various days. Dr. Siengalwicz, a Polish toxicologist and professor of forensic medicine of Lublin University, told me that they had identified, by chemical analysis, a total of 1,034 meters of human ashes recovered from graves and from near-by fields, which he estimated to represent the remains of perhaps 1,000,000 corpses.

The Soviet-Polish Commission of scientists and laymen, of which Dr. Siengalwicz was a member, was headed by Andrejez Vitos, then vice-president of the Polish Committee of National Liberation. It spent thousands of hours investigating the mountains of evidence, and its final report, covering every aspect of the camp, will doubtless be studied by pathologists, psychologists, criminologists and other scientists for years to come. Many of them, too, will probably refuse to believe it.

But not I, and not anyone who saw Maidanek and all the evidence of its horror. For us, nothing could erase the negative which re-created the whole picture in most convincing manner. This crowning achievement of Nazi totalitarianism, executed with German efficiency, was in a way far more frightening in its ultimate implications for mankind than the record of any rival killers in history.

The whole abattoir was still there when I went to Lublin at the end of August. The vast camp, enclosed by electrically charged barbed wire, the 200-odd barracks and buildings which were pens where transient human cattle were herded for slaughter, the chamber where they were gassed—they were open to public scrutiny now. Russians and Poles led their soldiers and recruits through the maze to indoctrinate them for battle. The open-air brick ovens fitted with electric blowers where corpses were cremated, the disinterred bodies of earlier victims—men, women and children killed by other means—and finally the tons of human ashes scattered about the fields in which the Nazis grew choice cabbages for their table. I saw all that.

I knew of course that faked evidence could sometimes appear very convincing, but years of experience with partisan propagandists had enabled me to smell out a "planted" scene as a mouse smells out a piece of cheese. Even when confronted with an obviously genuine atrocity, however, I often refrained from reporting it, simply because I had learned that there were always hundreds of people in America who would never believe man capable of such depravity and would start long correspondence with your editor, trying to prove that you were a fool or a liar.

One of history's most completely documented cases of rapine, torture and murder occurred at Nanking, in 1937, when the Japanese slew thousands of Chinese after taking the capital. The report on that atrocity was prepared by an international committee of highly respected American and European eye-witnesses, including doctors, professors and clergymen, and it was signed by the chairman, who happened to be a German Nazi whose Führer was allied with the Japanese. Nevertheless, hundreds of Americans obviously did not believe it. When I came home from China in 1941 many people referred to my quotations from that document and said, "That wasn't really true, was it?" Skepticism is a healthy thing, up to a point, but this was simply stupidity. It all seemed to go back somehow to the postwar debunking of reports about German baby-killers in Belgium. Since then many a misguided American has thought he was being sophisticated by refusing to believe the most irrefutable evidence of Nazi degeneracy.

But Maidanek was something different in my experience and it was something every decent person had to know about, because there was a point here of new and clinical interest. It was the diabolical system and efficiency of it, the comprehensive, centrally directed planning, that for the first time made a totalitarian modern industry out of the reduction of the human being from an upright ambulatory animal to a kilogram of gray ashes. No slaughterhouse was ever better organized for its purpose. All by-products were utilized. Nothing was wasted.

Everywhere in the chain of operations lay the characteristic hand of the German master of order, efficiency and economy, his complete absorption in the mechanics of the tasks before him, his rigid adherence to the principle of thoroughness in all things. It happened that two of my own great-grandparents were Germans, and from that side of my family I heard in my youth a great deal about those German virtues. Indeed, no one can say that American society has not benefited from them, either. But here at Lublin you got a complete perversion of the historic genius of a race, with method and means becoming everything, action completely dominating imagination, and the end itself losing all significance for the automatons bringing it about.

That was the phenomenon that fascinated me about Maidanek: the fact that it is perfectly possible to co-ordinate the utmost scientific order and means with the utmost barbarism of ends. Here human conscience was absolved of all guilt by the magic words "Orders from Berlin." "Kill! Kill! Kill!" screamed Goebbels for the record of all time. "Not you shall answer for this, but I." And the blockheads who listened to him spat on their hands and obeyed.

Nazi Death Plant

MAIDANEK was neatly laid out for killing, an impressive collection of buildings in a spacious setting. It had its own shops, its many miles of motor roads winding between high watch towers; it even had its own fire department. No one must burn before his time. In front of the residence of the commandant was a garden. Outside the camp offices was another garden. In the middle of it stood a ten-foot-high replica of a medieval castle which served as a fountain. It was built by Jewish prisoners, under the lash of Gestapo gangsters, from Jewish gravestones. In places you could still see the engraved Hebrew characters.

Prisoners sent to Lublin from all parts of Europe were instructed to bring everything they owned. They were to begin a new life in a "new settlement," some were told. Trustingly, they shipped their trunks of belongings, or relatives sent them, as instructed. Apparently none of these trunks ever saw the camp at all, but were unloaded in a Lublin warehouse—of which more later. In this way Hitler pried loose the last personal wealth of his victims.

Many had already been worked and starved into emaciation before reaching Maidanek and little labor power was lost through their segregation here. Even after they reached the camp, however, the still relatively able-bodied were held aside for more work. They helped to erect new buildings, which were constantly being added after August, 1941, until by 1943 the camp had a capacity of 40,000. When the sick and the lame fell exhausted at their labor, they were beaten and marked for speedy extermination.

Witnesses testified that various means were adopted to liquidate prisoners. The gas chambers could kill from 150 to 200 people in five minutes and were the main execution cells. Sometimes prisoners were clubbed or hanged. Sometimes SS men casually kicked or beat the life out of selected victims. German political prisoners were always shot, I was told by captured Nazis, while gas chambers were generally used for the others.

But Jews, Germans and other Europeans were all robbed in common and were all fed to the same ovens. The principle crematorium consisted of ten large ovens, with a capacity of some 1,400 bodies daily. Near the ovens still lay piles of tin urns. These were formerly used to receive ashes from the fires, which were then sold to people foolish enough to believe that they were buying the remains of their loved ones. Such filled urns netted the Nazis 5,000 Polish zlotys each. Nothing was wasted.

Not far from the Maidanek camp I visited some of the mass graves, where the victims of the Nazis had been buried in days before more efficient methods were adopted by the Gestapo. In the now opened pits lay hundreds of partly decomposed bodies of men, women, children and babies, many still wearing their rotting Polish and Russian native dresses. Some of the corpses had smashed skulls and were horribly mutilated and disfigured; others had been stabbed to death; some had bullet holes in them. It was an incredibly hideous sight and the stench was beyond description. From other graves, already emptied, the Nazis had removed corpses for cremation in the ovens of Maidanek, when the advance of the Red Army had threatened to expose the handiwork of the death factory. Their activity had been interrupted and never completed. A few minutes of it was all I could stand, but for days afterward the stink seemed part of my clothes.

At Maidanek, the bulk of the ashes was strewn upon the Nazis'

vegetable fields and the commandant's flower gardens. Gold
fillings were removed from the teeth of the corpses, and sometimes from live prisoners. Serviceable clothing was sent to the
large warehouse, converted from an unfinished theater owned
by the Catholic Church. Even rags were fumigated and preserved, for buttons and bits of cloth. And not far from the ovens
I saw the most sickening display of all, in this evidence of mass
murder.

Doubtless you have read about the building, some fifty feet
wide by one hundred feet long, which was devoted solely to old
shoes. Hundreds of thousands of pairs of them lay there, closely
packed down, footwear of every description, and each pair a
tragic history of a vanished owner. There were babies' tiny shoes
and children's boots, hundreds of them. There were little red
slippers, gold evening shoes, the high laced boots of an elderly
woman, the worn sandals of peasants, the frayed *valenki* of
Russians and Poles, rubbers from Akron—footwear from Paris,
Berlin, Vienna, Warsaw, Prague, Antwerp, Rotterdam, Madrid
and Moscow. Here mute testimony corroborated the evidence
of Nazi guards, the passports and other records I saw, that people from infants to octogenarians were wiped out. Most of all I
remember the shoe of a crippled woman, with a built-up sole
six inches high. Near by were a truss and a knee-length brace. All
these items had been kept for the shoemakers' old leather. Nothing was wasted.

Nothing Was Wasted

DOWNTOWN, in Lublin, a warehouse of four floors was filled
with the worn but fumigated intimate belongings of thousands
of people. Everything was carefully inventoried. There was a
section devoted to women's underclothing of all kinds, silk pan-
ties and brassières in one room, overcoats in another; corsets in
one department, stockings in another. One room was crowded
with children's garments, from swaddling clothes to woolen
knickerbocker suits. There was a corner piled high with babies'
cracked and chipped chamber pots.

I examined two trunks crammed with arch supporters, and
there were even wooden arms, legs, crutches and canes in various stages of wear. In one department I saw assorted medicines,
partly used tubes of toothpaste, old combs and vanity cases, nail
files and scissors. One whole shelf was devoted to children's
books and toys, smudged by small, loving hands.

"One day I saw 157 Polish children gassed to death," Hans
Stalp, a German prisoner who had been a guard at Maidanek,
told me. On another day, Nazi Officer Anton Thermos admitted
to us he had seen about 500 women and children gassed to death.
On a second occasion, he saw the bodies of 300 children taken
from the gas chambers.

Ledgers and stacks of inventory sheets were found in offices
of the warehouse. Down to the last spool of it, the Nazis knew
how much used thread they had on a given day. "Mention a date
and I'll tell you what was here," said the bespectacled Polish

theological student who rummaged through these files. "Well? Let us take March 31, 1944. Eighty thousand women's blouses; 160,089 pieces of assorted cloth; 316,000 pieces of ladies' underwear." And so on.

The file of Nazi correspondence produced interesting documentation from Berlin, the real pay-off in this novel factory-to-consumer industry. There were various orders for equipment for German settlers in the new empire conquered in Poland and the Ukraine. I saw a soiled letter from headquarters requesting garments for several thousand young supermen. The books were expertly kept, with German thoroughness. At the end of any day the commandant could advise Hitler just how many worn rompers and ladies' chemises were in stock, and how many had been shipped out. Who would have thought that supermen would stoop to rag-picking? But the motto was "nothing to be wasted."

Everything was taken care of here, everything but the last act. Incredibly, these industrialists of death, so systematic about everything else, neglected the one thing most important of all. At the last moment, they fled without completely destroying the evidence, and thus nullified all their previous elaborate efforts. Camp Commandant Thuman suddenly disappeared, and the remaining SS murder technicians were left *sans* Führer. Some kind of order must have finally come through from Berlin. Herr Moosveld, the crematorium Führer, managed to set fire to some of the abattoir buildings and to his own house, in which stood the bed where he had slept peacefully not ten feet from the incineration ovens. Winters are cold in Lublin, but Moosveld's quarters were very snug. He took his bath in water heated by the fires that burned his victims.

Yet it was a disorderly retreat. Enough evidence—far more than I can describe here—was left behind to incriminate everyone from Hitler to the dark little Obersturmführer, Theodore Scholen, a Nazi Party member and an SS man, whom the Russians inconveniently interrupted outside Lublin, on his way to Berlin. This fellow Scholen, to whom I talked, told of having frequently seen bodies carried through the camp. He recalled that from 18,000 to 20,000 people were killed on November 3, 1943—Belgians, Greeks, Italians and many others, besides a vast number of Jews, Poles and Russians. But it was only now, as he looked back on it all, that Herr Scholen realized that the whole thing was actually an extermination camp.

As for himself, Scholen stoutly maintained he had never taken part in the actual killings. He was kind to the prisoners. The most he admitted doing was the occasional removal of gold fillings from live prisoners' teeth, in search of hidden diamonds. But his extractions, he said, were always painlessly performed.

"Then who was actually responsible, Obersturmführer Scholen?" I asked him.

"Berlin," he answered, without batting an eye. Not the camp commandant, not Scholen, and none of the nineteen young idealists who once thought they were riding on the "wave of the future," and who worked under Scholen.

"We always acted on orders from Berlin," Scholen complacently explained. Didn't that make it all clear?

"Has it occurred to you that you yourself will be tried for your share in these crimes?" I asked him.

Ferret-like eyes blinked in astonishment. "That's absurd! I only carried out orders. As for a trial, I've done nothing. I'm absolutely blameless," concluded Scholen.

A year earlier I had been staying in a billet over in Scotland one night, listening to a young American flier just back from Italy, where he had been bombing the German lines. I heard him talk for some time with an RAF man who lay near us, in this vein: that he didn't believe all that "propaganda" about Nazi brutality; it was probably all lies.

"Why, I met some of their fliers we had captured, and they were fellows just about like us. Under other circumstances, you wouldn't mind introducing them to your girl. They say they are fighting for an ideal and they are ready to die for it, and that's just what we're doing. It's too bad to have to kill them."

We have toughened up a lot since then. Probably that young captain has, too, and I hope he read about Maidanek; it's tough on a man to have to kill fellow idealists and that might make it easier for him to sleep at night. But just as I expected, my editor got plenty of "it-couldn't-happen" letters from skeptical American amateur criminologists. From where they sat they knew it was all a Russo-Polish plot. The back of my hand to them. Sixteen quite hard-boiled American correspondents went to Maidanek and not one of us came away unconvinced. Not one of us shed a tear for Herr Scholen and his accomplices, either, when the Polish courts tried them some weeks later and hung them until dead.

Here is a macabre thing, though, that belongs in the unclassified paradoxes department. Weeks afterward, when I was in Moscow, the Lublin Poles sent a committee to visit the British and American ambassadors, presenting a list of Poland's relief needs. Most of the items were obvious necessities, but one request dumbfounded our diplomats. It read: *12 skeletons, for the Lublin University's medical laboratories.* The Poles explained that the Germans had destroyed or carried off all their pre-war skeletons.

IV

The Poles Apart

In Lublin, then headquarters of the Polish Liberation Committee and the Polish administrative committee which the Red Army had recognized as the sole authority on liberated Polish territory, I met Edward Boleslaw Osubka-Morawski for the first time. He later became vice-chairman of the new Polish Government which Moscow recognized soon after Warsaw was reoccupied. Here also I met General Boni Rola-Zimerski, head of the new Polish Army.

Rola-Zimerski gave a long detailed account of Red Army operations in which he had taken part, leading up to the capture of Praga, a suburb of Warsaw on the east bank of the wide Vistula River. He stated categorically that the Warsaw uprising, which was launched on the joint responsibility of the London Poles of the regime-in-exile, and General Bor, head of the underground Polish Home Army, was begun without prior consultation or liaison of any kind with the Red Army. He then explained that from what he, as leader of the Polish People's Army (a rival of the anti-Soviet Home Army), knew of Red Army plans, they had never included a frontal attack on Warsaw. He indicated that the Red Army would eventually take the Polish capital in an encirclement movement, and that the forces under General Bor, then fighting in Warsaw, were doomed to ultimate extermination by the Germans.

Later information, and real events, supported Rola-Zimerski's appraisal of the tragedy of Warsaw. The Germans had built up an extremely powerful defense system around the city; at one point as many as eighty separate lines of pillboxes and trenches were prepared. A near-crossing of the Vistula by the Russians, who had already paid a very heavy price to occupy Praga, could have been attempted only by a commander prodigal with the lives of his men; and even then that suicidal attempt might have failed. Wisely, the Red Army did not mount a further offensive till the following January, when the river had frozen hard and the marshes and swamps north and south of the capital gave a firm track for tanks and heavy-weapon carriers. Whether by chance or by design, this final move to complete the Red Army's liberation of Poland came also at a moment highly favorable for us, as it brought strategic aid to our beleaguered forces in Western Europe at the height of von Rundstedt's fierce counter-offensive into Belgium.

As Rola-Zimerski had predicted, Warsaw itself was by-passed and outflanked by the main Russian forces and its garrison eventually capitulated when it was entirely surrounded. But meanwhile the city had been leveled to the ground, the Polish Home Army had been destroyed, and several hundred thousand citizens had lost their lives in a hopeless and futile insurrection. Looking back now on the London Poles' fierce outcry that the Russians had "betrayed" them by not storming Warsaw and bringing salvation to General Bor, who had given the signal for a rising without even consulting our own chiefs-of-staff liaison in Britain, it seems clear that their own ineptitude of leadership and their fatally misguided sense of diplomacy were chiefly to blame.

In Poland itself the prestige of the exiled government rapidly disintegrated after the Warsaw fiasco. Hundreds of Bor's former officers began to join the new Polish People's Army. In Lublin we met two of the earliest of these disillusioned patriots to come over. One of them, Colonel Tarnova, had been commander of all Bor's Home Army security troops. He reported that even before the uprising he and many of his 2,500 officers had openly disagreed with Bor's plans for two sound military reasons: 1) their means were insufficient to the task; and 2) they had no understanding with the Red Army. Tarnova had, in fact, resigned his command and fled from Warsaw with the intention of reaching liberated Poland, where he had intended to communicate with (then) Premier Mikolajczyk of the regime-in-exile, to request him to postpone the uprising until liaison could be established with the Allies. It was, however, already too late to interfere when he reached Lublin. Now he agreed completely when General Rola-Zimerski declared:

"We are deeply convinced that Bor's order was given purely for political reasons. . . . The plan of the Home Army all along has been to appear suddenly in cities being occupied by the Red Army and only at the last moment, in order to assume power. Their mistake was that they thought they could operate in Warsaw independent of the will of the Red Army."

The Home Army's policy was thus the military reflection of the London Polish Government's political strategy, which continued to the last to refuse to recognize one basic and inescapable fact about the nation's destiny. It was simply that Poland could be restored to greatness only as a result of Red Army victory and heavy sacrifice of Russian blood. Therefore, only a government prepared to purge itself of all its anti-Soviet elements, and to co-operate fully with new pro-Soviet groupings bound to arise on the spot, in the wake of Russian victory, would be able to take power in the new Poland. Instead the London Poles steadfastly clung to a dozen myths and hopes rooted in their deep anti-Soviet prejudices and wish-fancies of the past, until at last Mikolajczyk left them and they lost the support of his Peasant Party, their most important political asset. From then on it was only a matter of time till Moscow—and after a decent face-saving interval, Britain and America—would recognize the new provisional Polish regime headed by Beirut and Osubka-Morawski, which later entered the ruins of Warsaw.

All this was already implicit in the conditions which existed when I first visited Poland. It was obvious also that the Polish Liberation Committee was, in reality, carrying out a political renovation so sweeping in character that it could only have been accomplished as a result of heavy revolutionary civil war had it not been done under the wings of the Red Army. Some aspects of civil war were present, anyway. Rola-Zimerski told us that his troops were disarming all members of the Home Army. Other Poles, attached to the Liberation Committee, admitted quite frankly that hundreds of their countrymen, who had refused to recognize the Committee's authority and still insisted on obeying only the radioed orders of the London government—which called for non-co-operation—were being interned as "enemies of the people." Remnants of the Home Army, hiding in the forests and villages, carried on a war of sabotage and assassination against both the Russians and their Polish allies.

The Polish Liberation Committee was then still weak and the four parties which had joined still needed the help of Miko-lajczyk's Peasant Party in order to command a mass following. But it was clear that their land-reform program would soon win a substantial base among the peasantry while their direct appeal to the urban workers would soon give them organized control of labor. No exiled government, depending on Anglo-American intervention, could long compete with such a regime on Polish soil. With the support which they knew would follow when Stalin actually turned over East Prussian and Silesian territory to Polish sovereignty, the political leaders of this first pro-Soviet regime in history had good reason to expect an early stabilization of the New Order whose foundations they were now busily laying in the tracks of the Red Army.

With liberated Poland and Rumania thus maturing as political prototypes, and the armistice terms imposed on other defeated Axis satellites available for study, it was already possible, by the autumn of 1944, to trace in broad outline the shape of things to come across the face of Eastern Europe—including, eventually, Germany. Let us examine this pattern that followed wherever the Red Army conquered.

CHAPTER FOUR

Red Star over Eastern Europe

I

120,000,000 New Friends

FROM the beginning of its struggle with the Axis the Kremlin called this "the Patriotic War of the Soviet Union." Russia was driven to war. She did not take the initiative for the purpose of bringing about ideological changes in the world, but she fought against men who wished to impose their ideology on her.

Nevertheless, Red victory inevitably alters the face of Europe. In the process of destroying her enemies, Russia has undoubtedly won millions of friends, or admirers, or at any rate a profound new respect, among peoples living near at hand. If before the war the peoples of Middle and Eastern Europe were led by regimes hostile to the Soviet Union, that was to a great extent made possible because of widespread underestimation of the real strength of the world's only socialist power. And if now Russia finds new friends in the very same places, the transformation is certainly born primarily out of experience with the prowess of Soviet arms.

The countries liberated by the Red Army together make up a large slice of Europe. They form a gigantic chain of territory averaging about 300 miles in width, with a frontier nearly 3,000 miles long as the much-traveled crow flies. They have an area, if we include Austria, East Prussia and Eastern Germany, of over a half million square miles. They had a pre-war population of over 120 million or some two-thirds as large as the Soviet Union.

What kind of future awaits these states? Upon what terms

58

are their new relationships with Russia being consolidated? Will the patriotic war merge into an ideological war for the advancement of socialism? Will Russia put her dearly won understandings with Britain and America in jeopardy by attempting to establish paramountcy of Communism? I was speculating about this one day with an elderly Communist, and this is what he said: "If any one had told me a few years ago that there would be no revolution in Eastern Europe after this war, I would have called that man crazy. But that's the way it is now. Russia above all wants stability in this part of the world and where the Red Army goes there will be no revolution."

It seemed true enough, if you applied traditional Marxist definitions of a working-class revolution. In the liberated lands beyond Soviet borders one saw no proletarian uprisings of the conventional pattern. There were no open exhortations to workers to overthrow the bourgeoisie; no demands for a "workers and peasants dictatorship"; no open denunciations of capitalism; no extravagant prophecies of an early Communist or socialist Europe. The familiar terminology of class warfare seemed almost to have disappeared from the lexicon of Europe's Leftists. If the Kremlin was fostering revolution it was doing so with a hand heavily gloved in velvet, and it was pointing rather than pushing.

"All the same," I said to this loyal Stalinist, "certain very interesting things are coming to pass. By whatever name you choose to give them, they mark a sharp revolutionary break with the past. Eastern Europe will never be the same again."

"But no one can say that the Comintern or the Soviet Government is bolshevizing these countries," he rejoined. "It is true the Red Army's victories have made many changes possible. But I say it is the people of those countries themselves who are getting rid of fascism and turning to the only possible form of government left to them."

It is a wide and fairly uniform pattern of adjustment—this "only possible form of government," which is becoming manifest from Finland and the Baltic states in the north, to the Adriatic

Sea on the southwest and to the frontiers of Turkey on the southeast. Eventually the pattern may reach into Greece. The end of the war finds Finland, Poland, Czechoslovakia, Yugoslavia, Rumania, Bulgaria, Hungary, Austria and Eastern Germany occupied by the Red Army—in most places in alliance with native anti-fascist forces. The amount of Europe under Russian occupation is thus far greater than at any time in history.

The way it looked from Moscow, all those nations and the many peoples within their changing boundaries were, without the violence and internal bloodshed of class war, going to realize a number of revolutionary reforms in common, more than they ever shared before. They would do so in a quiet, orderly manner, with excellent and stable police power, under the occupying forces, backing up the decrees of their own governments. There would be little barricade fighting to win this reformed new world. The fighting was done on the Volga and on the Don, the Dnieper, the Danube, the Vistula, the Oder and the Bug.

First on the list of reforms would be a fundamental reorientation in foreign policy. In this war all Russia's neighbors were mobilized or exploited by Germany to help her. It is the logic of Red Army triumph that any chance of a repetition of that experience will be effectively eliminated. Henceforth the Eastern European peoples will operate on the principle that warm friendship and collaboration with the Soviet fatherland are not only the best policy, but the "only possible" policy.

Observe further that Soviet frontier security will be enhanced not only by elimination of hostile land and air bases but by Russia's emergence as a first-class naval power. Henceforth the Red fleet will be the only sea power of consequence in the Baltic on the north and the Black Sea on the south. Russia will accept nothing less than equality in the Mediterranean also. It is hardly in keeping with her new commitments for the security of Europe that she should remain in any way dependent on Turkey, a power which showed little friendship for her in this war, for access to the Mediterranean. A showdown is coming for control of the Dardanelles. Stalin can wait because in this he cannot lose.

In Moscow I heard Polish, Rumanian, Czech and Finnish envoys of peace and the future unequivocally acknowledge the new era in the foregoing terms. And nowhere was the changed relationship of forces more frankly stated than in this manifesto issued by the Polish Liberation Committee, when it assumed administrative power in Poland: "History and the experience of the present war," said that model document, "show that *only the building up of a great Slav dam,** founded on Polish-Soviet-Czechoslovakian accord, can serve as a safeguard against the pressure of German imperialism. For 400 years constant conflicts between Poles and Ukrainians, Poles and Belorussians, Poles and Russians, have been the rule, to the detriment of both sides. Now a historic change has taken place in these relations. Conflicts are giving way to friendship and co-operation dictated by the mutual vital interests of these peoples. The friendship and fighting co-operation inaugurated by the brotherhood of arms of the Polish Army and the Red Army must be converted into a lasting alliance and neighborly co-operation after the war. . . . *An enduring alliance with our immediate neighbors—the Soviet Union and Czechoslovakia—will be the fundamental principle of Polish foreign policy.*"*

In hardly less decisive language Monsieur Patrascanu, the Communist head of the Rumanian Armistice Delegation, told me that it was "only through the closest collaboration and alliance with the Soviet Union that the Rumanian nation can arise again and that its independence and liberty can be guaranteed."

And beyond that feature, the basic feature of alliance between Eastern Europe and Russia? Again Poland and Czechoslovakia provide us with a guide to the future.

* Author's italics.

Economics of Reform

The second point nobody could mistake was that all fascists, fascist sympathizers, and all collaborationists, would be swept from these countries in a thorough and decisive manner. How would that work out in practice? "It will simply mean anybody," one foreign diplomat expressed it to me, "who doesn't agree with the pro-Soviet policy of the new governments." Was he right? Not entirely right because not inclusive enough.

Although the term "traitor to the people" had not been precisely defined, it would in most cases include all elements which stood in the way of realizing important *internal,* as well as *external,* reforms in policy. "Not a single German war criminal, not a single traitor to the Polish people, must escape punishment," said the Polish Committee's manifesto. "The frontiers of Poland will be closed to Hitler's agents and to those who betrayed Poland in September, 1939. . . . We will brush aside all mischief-makers and agents of reaction who, by trying to split national unity and foment internecine warfare among the Poles, are playing into the hands of Hitlerism."

Such "mischief-makers," inside and outside Poland, would not enjoy democratic liberties, nor even rights of citizenship promised to other Poles. Nor would they enjoy rights of property ownership. Similarly, the Czech Government planned to punish traitors and collaborationists by depriving them of their property as well as by other means, I was told by F. Memec, Minister Plenipotentiary and head of the Czechoslovakian Administrative

Delegation which assumed power in the liberated Czech territory.

We have seen how in Rumania the new administration likewise began by retaining control of industry used to support the Hitlerite war. Yugoslavia and Bulgaria adopted similar plans. In several countries the liquidation of the Germans and the confiscation of German property would in itself automatically establish state ownership over the largest industrial enterprises. Nearly all the heavy industry in Poland and Czechoslovakia, for instance, was already under German control before the attack on Russia. And after the Nazi occupation virtually all important smaller capitalists either were robbed outright of their enterprises or, if they collaborated, were compelled to take in Nazi partners. Those who were forced to "sell out" to the Germans would never fully re-establish their rights of ownership. As for those who fell in line with German war aims: they would now be regarded as "traitors to the people." Their property, if not their lives, would be forfeited.

Methods adopted for utilizing confiscated industrial plants in the liberated countries would vary. In Rumania I had found that absentee-owned factories were provisionally operated by committees of workmen, while ownership and control remained with the state. In Poland Osubka-Morawski told me that expropriated industrial plants were being operated by state boards which included representatives of labor.

"Some factories taken over in this way," Osubka-Morawski said, "may be returned to their previous owners, and property of traitors may be sold to other private persons, if there is a market for them. But all *industry of national importance will be owned by the state.** We are in favor of placing all industry under government control. We also want to encourage private enterprise wherever possible, but there will be government regulation of all production and distribution."

It ought to be remembered that in all the Baltic states, in

* Author's italics.

Czechoslovakia, Rumania and other Balkan countries, but above all in Poland, a vast amount of enterprise and land no longer had legitimate claimants. The former owners were murdered by the Nazis. Two to three million Jews, some of them extremely wealthy people, as well as many non-Jewish capitalists, were obliterated or driven from Europe. Debt problems were also somewhat simplified, owing in part to the liquidaton of thousands of money-lenders and pawnbrokers. Inflation will wipe out the rest.

Osubka-Morawski predicted that some of the shops and small enterprises taken back from the Germans would be made into co-operatives. Employees would be assisted by the state to become owner-operators. And this seemed likely to happen in other formerly Nazi-occupied countries.

A third point about Eastern Europe was that national minority questions would be settled by direct negotiation between neighboring states, including constituent republics of the USSR, rather than by plebescites or international arbitration. German minorities would likely be given no choice except a return to what remained of the Fatherland, or to hard labor in the countries they despoiled. The precedent was set by the September agreement between the Polish Liberation Committee and the Ukrainian and Belorussian Soviet Republics. They provided for mutual evacuation of Poles from Russia and of Ukrainians and Belorussians from Poland.

The agreement for exchange of populations was an omen of the future equally as important as the Polish-Russian military alliance itself. It meant that Stalin would not countenance continuation of the old situation, in which émigré Russian colonies in other lands had been exploited by anti-Soviet governments for purposes inimical to stability and peace. Further, it liquidated one fundamental basis of agitation carried on by the anti-Soviet Poles abroad—the claims of Polish land barons to the Western Ukraine. But of that, more later.

We are reminded that there was also a Rumanian minority in

Soviet Moldavia, while Ukrainian minorities lived in Rumania and Czechoslovakia. The Soviet-Polish agreement would likewise form a model for solution of minority disputes between Rumanians and Hungarians in Transylvania, Czechs and Poles in Silesia, and so on. It was obvious that Hungarians would be moved out of Transylvania, along with the Germans from Rumania. The interesting point was the fundamental nature of the solutions and their historic permanence.

Fourth, in Poland and Czechoslovakia, and in other cases in Eastern Europe also, the liberated states would be encouraged to demand reparations from Germany. The aim was to commit all these former Axis satellites to new frontiers acquired at the expense of Prussians and with Soviet patronage. Polish antifascists now coming to power wanted not only East Prussia and Silesia, but also a share of Germany industry. Osubka-Morawski told me that Poland would take over as much German machinery as she could get, not only in East Prussia but anything available to her in Germany.

What scope did this leave for the introduction of new capital from abroad? It seems that most of the countries I have mentioned will welcome foreign investments, except in land. But government responsibility for production will everywhere be very broad. It is at any rate clear that in Poland and Czechoslovakia any foreign investment will necessarily take on the form of a contract with the state, and be worth no more than the stability of the regime in power.

Fifth, "There won't be any large estates left in Poland," Morawski stated quite categorically, *"except for land owned by the Church."* And how long even individual churches themselves will hold on to their estates is uncertain. When I attended a peasant Youth meeting in Poland, delegates there were demanding Church land, too. They were much more radical than the Polish Committee itself. But Osubka-Morawski and the various parties behind him were proceeding cautiously and only as far

* Author's italics.

as, they claim, the 1921 Constitution authorized them to go. Church property would not be touched. Inside the Committee it was the Socialists who were insisting on ultra-radical reforms, such as collectivization and state ownership of all industry, while the Communists (in the Workers Party) were the restraining, conservative influence.

A land fund was set up in Poland under a Department of Agriculture and Agrarian Reform. This fund was first capitalized by the acquisition of farm implements, machinery and livestock, and by confiscation of "the land of Germans, traitors to the Polish people, and landed estates of over fifty hectares." In the case of lands taken from the Reich—Silesia and East Prussia—which the Poles plan to re-incorporate into the new state, individual landowners would be permitted to retain estates as large as one hundred hectares.

Some areas were set aside as model farms, to be operated as enterprises of the Polish state. The bulk of the land was divided among "small and middle peasants, small tenant farmers with large families, and agricultural laborers . . . taking as a basis five hectares of arable land for the average family."

On the whole it was safe to say that Osubka-Morawski's prediction of an end for all large estates in Poland would apply in all countries of Eastern Europe. Czechs of the Administrative Delegation told me that most of the Sudeten Germans would probably be expropriated and their lands divided among loyal citizens. Similar treatment would be given to all other landowners, whether absentee or resident, who had collaborated with the Nazis. And after the Bucharest *coup d'État*, George Popp, Secretary General of the Rumanian National Peasant Party, told me that property of the half million German minority in Rumania would be expropriated and divided among Rumanian peasants. All other large estates would be liquidated, leaving only the Church and Crown in possession of farms tilled by tenants.

One could already foresee that the remaining large estates in Bulgaria and Yugoslavia would be similarly liquidated. Some holdings, possibly later to prove forerunners of modified collectivization, would in each case be retained for development of state farms, as in Poland.

When the Red Army reached Hungary toward the end of 1944, Hungarian Communists in Moscow drew up a program somewhat similar to that of the Polish Committee, to be adopted by the new government which the Kremlin would presently recognize. In October it was already rumored that an agreement had been reached between the Hungarian underground leaders and the Red Army. Hoping to get some clue to the anti-fascist Hungarians' plans, I attended a public lecture one evening in October, when C. Rakoshi, a recognized Communist authority on Hungary, spoke before a packed hall. Lectures of this nature were not frequent in war-time Russia and were given only for a calculated political purpose. As it was certain that Rakoshi's speech had been carefully scrutinized and approved in advance by the Soviet Propaganda Bureau, his manner of expression was of great interest.

"Why is Hungary chained to Germany?" the speaker asked. "The explanation lies in the internal structure of the country. Power is centered in the hands of reactionary landlords, and the agrarian situation is similar to that which existed in Tsarist Russia in 1917: on the one hand, the reactionaries, landowner-magnates; on the other, the landless peasantry, the democratic forces. Landowners seek to hold their estates at any price and this makes them incapable of acting in the interest of the nation."

Rakoshi attributed the weakness of democratic forces in Hungary to the fact that "the working-class leadership, the Communist Party" had been forced underground for twenty-six years and thus "the democratic movement lacked a mainspring." Nevertheless, the people of Hungary were essentially democratic. "Developing events" would soon wipe out the dictatorship, and "the working class will act as the motor of the future struggle against fascism." A new Hungary would arise, "the foremost task of which will be the establishment of friendly relations with the victorious Soviet Union." And, needless to say, the liquidation of the "reactionary landlords." And "developing events" did, indeed, soon make prophetic the succinct words of Comrade Rakoshi.

So much for economic foundations. What of the political composition of these new anti-fascist governments? Without attempting to discuss this in terms of party labels, certain tendencies can be clearly observed.

·◦[ ]◦·

III

Politics of Change

The provisional Polish administration frankly stated that democratic liberties could not be exercised by "traitors to the people," a term which, in many ways, was curiously reminiscent of the old Marxist expression, "class enemies of the state."

It was evident from the Polish Committee's manifesto that most, if not all, of the landlords connected with the pre-1939 Polish Government were considered "traitors to the people." In varying degrees, that could apply to other pre-1939 governments of Eastern Europe, as well as to outright fascist collaborators. It could also be taken for granted that émigré landlords and capitalists generally would find their personal histories closely scrutinized when they sought readmission to their native lands after the war.

Whose stock, then, would stand highest in the post-war political life of this vast region? What was the sound stuff on which the state could be rebuilt? First of all the peasant, the man who fed the nation. Secondly, the worker, the man who produced goods for use and lived on his wages. Thirdly, the partisan and the soldier, the men and women and youths who stayed on their own soil and uncompromisingly fought the invader.

In the third group were found some surviving intellectuals and professional people. Also in this category belonged many of the clergy, many small business men, and some small bureaucrats, who managed to work under the Germans without betraying their people. Such men suffered heavily during the occupation and thousands were destroyed.

In Rumania, a few weeks after Red Army occupation, trade unions quickly revived, until ninety percent of all workers were organized. In liberated Poland the organization of labor and revival of trade unions was not only legalized but officially sponsored. *Polpress*, official news agency of the Polish Provisional State Administration, publicly announced that "the department of labor, social welfare and public health has set out to organize (sic) trade unions." Peasant unions also were organized by members of the Government. Obviously they were not being drilled to doff their caps to returning landowners and capitalists backing the London Poles.

An outgrowth of intensified labor-union organization in Poland was likewise seen in the increased following of the new pro-Soviet Socialist Party, as led by another member of the Provisional Government, Dr. Boleslav Drobner. It was noteworthy that all important members of the Polish regime were themselves either of peasant or worker origin—though they were not all Communists, as suggested abroad. And here you could discern a sixth characteristic likely to be found in future government, not only in Poland but in other neighbor states of Russia. *This was that not land barons and capitalists, but organized peasants and organized workers, as led by leftist political parties, friendly to Russia, would win all power.*

Seventh, freedom of press, speech, assembly and worship would more closely parallel the Soviet definition of those rights than the Anglo-Saxon parliamentary conception. The Polish

Committee solemnly proclaimed "the restoration of all democratic liberties, equality of all citizens without distinction of race, creed or nationality, freedom to form political and trade-union organizations, freedom of press and conscience." But wrong-minded people were warned that "democratic liberties must not be allowed to serve enemies of democracy."

In still other respects the Polish program obviously would be echoed beyond Polish frontiers. It called for improved wage standards and modern labor legislation, extension of social-welfare institutions of all kinds, enforcement of compulsory education, immediate housing for the neediest section of the population, and wide fostering of co-operative societies.

Prime Minister Muraviev, when he led Bulgaria in its complete somersault from the camp of the Axis into the fold of the Allies, consulted Bulgarian Communists and then announced a series of reforms which strikingly resembled the Polish Committee's manifesto. He pledged to restore all the people's democratic freedoms, abolish racial discrimination, renew all constitutional rights, release all political prisoners, dissolve all fascist organizations, and even to "end the embezzlement of national property." Muraviev's Government did everything but prescribe punishment for itself as "traitor to the people." That omission caused its collapse—and it was promptly remedied the following day by its successor, the Government of Georgiev, who ordered Muraviev's arrest.

Bulgaria finally comprehended that it was expected she should not only disown her unsavory erstwhile associates, but should join in the drive to exterminate them. Only when the overthrow was complete, only when measures were enforced to arrest and expropriate adherents of all regimes formed after the end of 1940, only when Bulgaria was ready to make war on Germany, was it possible to find a common ground with the Soviet Union.

Naturally one should not draw parallels too closely in the countries I have mentioned. They are in important respects on quite different levels of development. It is apparent, for example, that the extremely sound and politically mature people of a state like Czechoslovakia, which will be one of Europe's foremost industrial powers after the war, will much more quickly recover stability than a country like Rumania, full of illiterate peasants and corrupt officials, or a state like Poland, with its sharp class conflicts and its endless party quarrels.

IV

Nazism Destroys Capitalism

So WHAT was emerging was a pattern much along lines urged by Communists and some other parties of the Left, before and after Munich. From 1933 on, European Communists generally abandoned their earlier slogans of proletarian revolution. Instead they sought to unite with liberals and democrats everywhere, first to form popular-front and later on united-front governments, to include all parties to resist the rise of fascism. They failed then. Today the popular front seems the logical heir to power, born above the grave of fascism, and fully backed by Soviet victory.

Obviously it will depend to a considerable extent on the wisdom and moderation of the various Communist parties whether or not the popular front acquires vigor and growth as the political child of the future. So far Communists in Rumania, Czechoslovakia, Poland, Bulgaria, Hungary and Yugoslavia have behaved cautiously and with political astuteness. To date they have contented themselves with fewer positions of power than the real relation of forces might justify.

In 1945 the progress chartered by all the provisional anti-fascist regimes seemed to be growing out of the logic of changed conditions brought about largely by processes of the war itself, rather than by a series of decrees based on ideological preconceptions forced upon an unwilling populace. In the irony of history it has turned out that Nazism was thus the instrument which, setting out to overthrow Communism, succeeded in destroying the structure of laissez-faire capitalism throughout Europe. And in its crash Nazism is taking down with it the remnants of economic and social feudalism which inevitably harnessed themselves to Hitler.

That isn't the whole picture of the new deal coming to Eastern Europe, and it is only one man's interpretation. But I think in its crude outline it is fairly accurate. It is the interpretation which, in the main, I cabled home while I was still in Russia. And again it rather surprised me that it passed Soviet censorship—which is frankly political in its inhibitions, as well as military. I took it to mean that Moscow was not trying to hide its preferences, nor their implications, from the outside world.

But Russia's plans for Germany and Austria, discussed in a later chapter, were another matter. Before attempting to scrutinize them it would be well to see something more of what the war has cost the Soviet peoples, and of the bill they are to present to Hitler's heirs. A good place to study that was the Ukraine, the scene of Hitler's greatest attempt at "colonization"—and of his greatest defeat.

CHAPTER FIVE

Ukraine: In the Wake of Conquest

I

Items in the Bill

WHEN I had left the Soviet Union, in 1943, most of the Ukraine was still in Nazi hands. Since then the whole valley of the Dnieper had been freed. Kiev itself, the ancient and picturesque citadel of the Southern Slavs, which was an outpost of European civilization a millennium ago, had been in Soviet hands more than a year. Yet it was not till I went on a sobering journey into this twilight of war that I fully realized the price which 40,000,000 Ukrainians paid for Soviet—and Allied—victory. The whole titanic struggle, which some are so apt to dismiss as "the Russian glory," was first of all a Ukrainian war. No fewer than 10,000,000 people had been "lost" to the Ukraine since 1941, I was told by a high Ukrainian official. That excluded men and women mobilized for the armed forces.

A relatively small part of the Russian Soviet Republic itself was actually invaded, but the whole Ukraine, whose people were economically the most advanced and numerically the second largest in the Soviet Union, was devastated from the Carpathian frontier to the Donets and Don rivers, where Russia proper begins. No single European country suffered deeper wounds to its cities, its industry, its farmlands and its humanity.

We may have forgotten how large a role American engineers and machinery played in the industrialization of this Republic, but the Ukrainians have not. Today they hope for renewed American industrial help. The post-war Soviet market for American goods is to a major extent a Ukrainian market. To the same degree the heaviest Soviet war claims against Germany are Ukrainian claims. And in the mind of every Soviet diplomat, when he talks about post-war Europe, is the thought that this union's Ukrainian frontier must be flanked by such dependable structures of security that the cataclysm cannot be repeated.

Because of that, if for no other reason, we should become more familiar with the Ukrainian people, or Little Russians, who have their own language and culture and history, older than that of Great Russia. And possibly partly because of that also I found an extraordinary spirit of cordiality and frankness in the Ukraine, and an almost unique readiness to supply facts and figures where they seemed available.

The rest of the USSR is fifty times the size of the Ukraine, but the Ukraine held about half the giant nation's pre-war key industry. One district alone produced more pig iron and steel than Japan, Belgium, Italy and Poland taken together. Ukrainian mines supplied half the hard coal and three-fourths of the coking coal for the entire Soviet Union. The Ukraine produced sixty-two percent of Soviet iron ore and its bauxite mines furnished seventy percent of pre-war Soviet aluminum.

At Zaporozhe, on the Dnieper, Soviet engineers put into operation the largest electrical-power station in Europe. By 1941, Ukrainian electrical energy was twenty-four times greater than the amount developed in 1913, and the output of Ukrainian metal-working industries had increased thirty-four times. With the aid of 100,000 tractors, the well-stocked Ukrainian farms were highly mechanized. Ukrainian agriculture was ninety-nine percent collectivized and it grew a fifth of the nation's wheat and more than a third of its sugar beets. Its farms were among the most prosperous in Europe.

No wonder Hitler believed that if he could close his fist over the black soil of the Ukraine he could force Russia to her knees. If he had been allowed to take over all this muscle and power intact, then he might indeed have been far more successful. But as early as July 3, 1941, Stalin decided to apply a scorched-earth policy where it proved impossible to carry means of production to the rear. When the Red Army blew up the great Dnieprostroi power project in August, 1941, a painful sigh spread over Russia; but it was a necessary act. It not only greatly delayed the Nazi advance but made it impossible for the enemy to operate the tremendous industrial complex around Dnepropetrovsk, just as similar sabotage rendered the rich Donets Basin practically useless to the invaders.

From other Ukrainian cities many thousands of tons of machinery were moved eastward, to become the nucleus of new plants set up in Siberia and Central Asia. In most cases, such machinery will remain where it is. Ukrainian leaders count little on it for direct replacements—though some of it will reproduce itself to help restore its former hearth and home.

However, the more or less orderly evacuation of such vital movable machinery and the demolition of many key plants were only the beginning of the war's cost to the Ukraine. The Red Army had to withdraw hastily and leave the greater part of the industry behind. From all occupied areas, according to Soviet figures, the Government managed to evacuate, by heroic measures, a total of 1,200,000 railway carloads of industrial equipment, of which only a part came from the Ukraine. Compared with the Nazi pillage during their two years' occupation, the Russians saved a modest amount. Cruel and finally fatal blows were delivered by the invaders to the basis of Ukrainian industry and mechanized agriculture late in 1943 and 1944. In Kiev, for example, only one of a half dozen great cities of the Ukraine, the Nazis not only carried off all the machinery but stripped every house and office of its last piece of furniture. The mayor of Kiev told me that about 250,000 cars were utilized in that operation alone.

Standing in the midst of the ruins of the great Bolshevik machine-building plant, the engineer-in-chief told me that it would cost 20,000,000 gold rubles to replace the lost machinery in this one spot. Incidentally, he thought it would take 2,500 workmen from two to three years to clear away the debris and rebuild the structure. I found that 8,000 Russian prisoners of war had been employed at the plant, for two months prior to the Nazi retreat, solely in dismantling machinery and packing it for shipment to Germany, where Hitler was desperately attempting to restore his own bomb-ravaged war industries. Multiply that by hundreds, by thousands, and you get an idea how much labor, how much time and thought, and how many million freight cars the Germans devoted to the denudation of the Ukraine.

Commissions were still adding up the total damage. Meanwhile, Vladimir Nikolaievich Valuyev, the able and plain-speaking young chairman of the Ukrainian Gosplan, or State Planning Commission, let me sample a few rough estimates. For instance, in the town alone, about 22,000,000 square meters of living space were destroyed. In Poltava, a typical rural district, about 100,000 peasant homes were gone, out of an original total of 362,000. In a single industro-agrarian region, Kamenets-Podolsk, 470,000 civilians were killed and 103,000 were deported to Germany, out of an original 2,000,000 population; 562 villages were destroyed, with 18,000 peasant homes and 6,000 *kolkhoz* buildings; and 310,000 horses and cattle and 1,700 tractors were carried off. One Soviet authority stated that at least fifty percent of all the means of Ukrainian livelihood and production were gone. In the case of Dnepropetrovsk alone, the replacement cost in such terms will run to 350,000,000 American dollars.

Pierre Cot, the Frenchman who made an extensive tour of the liberated areas for the de Gaulle Government, gave me 250,-000,000,000 gold rubles, or $50,000,000,000, as his estimate of the damage done to Russia during the war. That includes only physical plant, of course. If it is near the truth, then one might guess the Ukrainian part at somewhere between $30,000,000,000 and $40,000,000,000. And the mechanical equipment needed to restore it might then cost something like $10,000,000,000.

II

The Wasteland

ABOUT half the Ukraine lying on the west bank of the Dnieper was liberated only in the spring and summer offensives of 1944, but the greater industrial and farming areas came back into Soviet hands again late in 1943. I wanted to know what had been accomplished in a year's effort at recovery and I took the question to several Ukrainian authorities and made spot investigations at a number of farms and factories around Kiev. I did not find anybody minimizing the tasks or inclined to exaggerate what had been done. I sensed a good deal of impatience with clumsy propaganda attempts to convince the outside world that full-scale "reconstruction" had already begun. Everywhere there was emphasis on the complexity of the difficulties, the volume of work to be done.

Despite that, what emerged out of my inquiry, and what is perhaps the main message of this report, was something else. It was that the Ukraine seems likely to recover its former position more quickly than any other war-torn country of Europe. It was that not long after Ukrainian industrial production has been fully restored, the Soviet Union may be much farther along the road toward abundance than it was before 1941.

But right now there was the bleak present. There was the labor shortage. The millions of Ukrainians taken to Germany included many of the nation's best workers. Some went eastward, and many will remain there. In one factory I found only 220 workers out of an original 6,000 were back at work. In another, thirty answered to the foreman's roll call of 700. In the small industries and workshops, most of the workers had been Jews. A million and a half Ukrainian Jews once lived here, but little trace of them now remains.

On the farms there were even fewer men than in towns. At one collective 264 workers, out of a pre-war total of 700, had reappeared, but only fifteen men were back, out of an original 234. A second farm had supported 2,035 peasants before the war. Now it mustered only forty-five able-bodied men out of its former 1,400. A different way of saying the same thing was that out of 3,900 tractor drivers trained here in 1944, 3,500 were women. The dean of the Ukrainian University, many of whose buildings were blown up by the Nazis before they left, told me he had 2,300 students back in the improvised classrooms. Only 400 were males.

I met a Russian feminist on the train, and a feminist is rather a *rara avis* in this country. "The men only have to fight, but we have to feed the Army and clothe it and nurse it and arm it and protect the next generation all at once," she said. "Now we have to pick up the pieces here and rebuild the place and provide the future with new sons and daughters. They say this is a man's war, but there has never in history been anything that was more of a woman's war. No wonder we hate war more than men do!"

Women were doing most of the salvaging and the amount of labor involved in cleaning up after a demolition is seldom appreciated. There were few tools or wheels left. At one former factory I watched hundreds of women and boys working with bare hands trying to clear the debris from a corner of the plant. It seemed to me they were engaged on a lifetime task.

"It doesn't work out like the reverse moving pictures," dourly remarked the engineer with me. "Now, if some smart lad would just invent a bomb to put a building together again . . ."

But even if good labor and materials were available, reconstruction would be severely hampered by lack of other means.

Transport, for instance. Formerly, Ukrainian government institutions owned tens of thousands of trucks; now they had but a
few thousand broken-down lorries. Railways and bridges had
been restored only to the minimum necessary to maintain military supply. In farm work the shortage was also severe. Seventy
percent of the tractors and eighty percent of the horses were
missing.

Beyond that, the lack of materials of all kinds was acute.
Everything went to the Army first, if it was of any military value.
Ukrainian electrical-power, coal, iron, steel and chemical industries were destroyed almost totally, and the major work of
restoration had hardly begun. One reason was that a very large
part of Ukrainian enterprise must remain immobilized until the
great dams on the Dnieper were rebuilt and until the Donbas
mines were working again. Some rosy pictures had been painted
abroad about that. But in fact Dnieprostroi was still a ruin.
Ukrainian officials told me that so far production in the Donbas,
too, was insignificant.

"Don't forget that the Donbas hasn't been worked for three
years, and that it was ninety-seven percent mechanized," I was
reminded by the Gosplan Chief, Valuyev, "and all that mechanization was lost. The mines are still flooded with 350 million cubic
meters of water, and it keeps piling in at the rate of thirty-five
million cubic meters every day. Our pumps aren't big enough
for the job. About all we can do is to hold the water at its present
level. We won't be able to clear the mines again until we can
import some big pumps from America—likely not till after the
war."

Few machine tools were being turned out, and few tools meant
little new machinery. One example: the pre-war Kharkov tractor
plant had 1,100 machine tools and made a hundred tractors a
day. Now the same plant had a hundred machine tools and made
three tractors a day. The "restored" plant in demolished Stalingrad could assemble and repair, but could not manufacture
machines.

Why couldn't the needed machinery be made in the East—I wanted to know—by all that new industrial plant in Siberia and Asia? The answer I got was that the first priority was still the defeat of Germany. Secondly, there was the demand for equipment to complete planned industry becoming a permanent fixture in the East. In many lines help could be expected only after the war.

III

The Job Begins

For all that, the Ukrainians had in a single year, using little but their hands and feet, it seemed, turned their country from a complete liability back into an important producer of the Soviet Union. Here are the skeletal facts of the achievement—the triumphs, largely, of women and children and old men coming out of holes in the ground, after three years of terror and war:

First, there was that amazing 1944 harvest. Big areas were still battlefields, but everything possible was planted, including earth not yet de-mined—and some peasants paid with their lives for that. Everything that would pull a plow or a cultivator, a harrow or a reaper, was utilized. Around Kiev, 40,000 cows were harnessed up. All citizens, including part of the Army, were mobilized to bring in the harvest. Seventy percent of the crop was reaped by sickle and scythe. By late October the Ukrainian wheat yield was found to be three-fourths of a normal pre-war harvest, covering more than sixty percent of the area sown in 1940.

Secondly, while Ukrainian workmen stayed in the East, Ukrainian cattlemen and collective chiefs drove back such stock as they had earlier managed to evacuate. These returning migrants were thinly spread across the Republic. By the end of 1944 nearly eighty percent of the Ukrainian collectives had already restored some kind of cattle-breeding sections: half of them had pigs again, a third had sheep, two-thirds had poultry.

In the autumn of 1944, the Ukrainian commissariat of agriculture began to mobilize farmers to rebuild their houses. By November, more than 100,000 had been erected. Throughout the relatively mild Ukrainian winter this work continued.

"We lacked tools, nails, glass and transport," explains the vice-chairman of the region, who stood by my side as I watched work proceeding on one of the 500 rebuilding projects in the province of Kiev. "We lack all kinds of finished materials, but we have an abundance of good timber everywhere, we have some fine old carpenters among the peasants, we have technique, and our people are crying for houses."

Combining those advantages and hurdling the obstacles, the commissariat went ahead with plans immediately. The state set up model housing projects where peasants could come, look and learn how to build the same thing in their village. The models were five or six rooms in the old New England style, put together joint by joint, made from top to bottom with little but an ax and a rip saw, covered with thick grass roofs, and requiring very few nails. The peasants were allowed to cut the timber they needed from the state forests and were helped with transport. Any home builder was entitled to a 10,000-ruble loan from the Government without interest, to pay for labor, materials and furniture. By the new technique, fifteen hands could erect one house in a month.

"How soon do you expect to get a roof over the heads of all your people?" I asked Starchenko, the cheerful, round-faced vice-chairman of the Government.

He listed all the impediments to rapid achievement. "Given a little luck, we ought to have a roof for everybody in a year and a half or two years."

It would be wrong to leave the impression that industry wasn't producing here, too; though most of the restored floor space you saw seemed to be empty and waiting for machinery—American machinery, the Ukrainian at your side often hastened to add. For one thing, about a third of all the pre-war industrial-power facilities of the Republic was back in use—a fine accomplishment.

Also, by the end of 1944, twenty-two mines were drained in the Krivoi Rog, thirty-seven open-hearth furnaces were restored, twenty-three steel-rolling mills had been rehabilitated and in excess of 500 workings of coal mines were operating. In terms of pre-war output, their significance was still negligible, according to Valuyev, but I happened to know that was more blast furnaces than the Chungking Government of China had built in six years.

Kiev's industry produced in 1944 about an eighth of its 1940 output. Enough light industry was restored elsewhere to enable state planners to count on a 1945 production of around fifteen to twenty percent of 1940. But even in 1945, eighty-five percent of the emphasis would be on repair and construction of buildings, only fifteen percent on machinery.

People who were running the Ukrainian economy thought that despite the good harvest the bread ration couldn't be increased much in 1945. The Army had to be fed for a long time and the cities would be filling up with bread-eaters needed to rebuild. A half million souls were back in Kiev already. Another thing was that the average Russian would probably get little more sugar for a couple of years yet. By high-priority concentrated effort, the Ukrainian beet-sugar industry could be got back to normal earlier, but it wasn't yet on the cards stacked up in the offices of the state planning commission.

IV

Reasons for Hope

DESPITE such dark patches on the canvas, or perhaps because of them, the astute group of young men and women who were putting this place together again expected Ukrainian agriculture to be back on both feet in two to three years. They believed both heavy and light industry would recover the 1940 level of production within five years after the end of the war. Even the Donbas and Dnieprostroi will be restored within that time. Cities would take longer to reconstruct. All kinds of new standards were being enforced; they would be more beautiful and more efficient. But cities, too, would be rebuilt in eight to ten years—with the help of German prisoners. About the only thing these young people would not predict with reasonable confidence was the probable recovery of pre-war population.

As I talked to thirty-six-year-old Valuyev, who had spent all his adult life as an economic planner, he suddenly produced from his desk the translation of an article of mine. It was called "How Fast Can Russia Rebuild?"* It was published in February, 1944, but the war mails were slow, and Mr. Valuyev had just read it.

"What's wrong with it?" I asked him. He didn't agree with one of my political comments—I would have been astounded if he had—but as for the treatment of reconstruction and the prospects of recovery, he said it was about right. "It's a correct interpretation of the role of foreign trade in our post-war economy."

* *Saturday Evening Post.*

I am bestowing this accolade on myself because some reader may wish to go back to that article for an analysis, which I won't repeat here, of the reasons why Soviet industry may fully recover within five years after the war. The earlier report had explained why human needs inexorably would be subordinated to the replacement of heavy and reproductive basic industry. I emphasized that under the complete control of the state monopoly, the fundamental aim of Soviet foreign trade is not large or small imports or exports *per se*, but only the exchange needed to achieve the complete and speedy "techno-economic independence" of the USSR. Because of that, American business should not expect a permanent "panacea market" in Russia.

Valuyev stressed that, in accordance with this conception, the Ukraine and the Soviet Union required from the United States machine tools and basic means of production and the means of transportation and mechanization rather than consumers' goods. The needs are urgent and tremendous, as we have seen. How the imports will be paid for is not so apparent. That is the problem of Mr. Mikoyan, of the Foreign Trade Commissariat in Moscow.

For the new "autonomy" law does not, of course, enable republics like the Ukraine to make direct trade agreements with foreign states, or to plan independently of the center. State planning is much too complex and comprehensive for that. Where the solutions to the production and reconstruction problems of each farm or shop are co-ordinated not only within towns and districts and provinces but among republics and across the vast stretches of the Soviet Union, there can be no more regional economic independence than there can be any scope for "free enterprise."

Plans in wartime were flexible and on a semi-annual basis. But these, too, were filtered into three-year and five-year plans leading into the peace, and with still broader plans looking far into the future. Whatever else they might not have, at the moment, the top Soviet economic planners had something in their desk drawers that no other country had. They had a pretty accurate outline of what they would have in this country a decade from now.

The realm of diplomacy seemed to offer wider scope for the exercise of such Ukrainian autonomy as existed, however, and this was notably so in the Republic's relations with neighbor Poland. I asked Vice-Chairman Starchenko about the agreement between the Ukraine and Poland and whether there had been any mutual transfer of Ukrainian and Polish populations from their respective territories. He told me these exchanges had rapidly gone ahead. By mid-November about 300,000 Ukrainians, out of a possible 450,000 in Poland, had already returned to this Republic. Starchenko said that Poles had been going back across the frontier, too, "in considerable numbers." I was interested to hear that the evacuation included Lvov, long the center of a tug of war. This news was not released at Moscow for some weeks later, however—when the physical "depopulation" of the Ukraine of its Poles was already a *fait accompli.*

To all this discussion I want to add one or two observations to balance the picture against the rest of Russia. First, it ought to be clear that though the war has brought ruin to the occupied areas, it has been the making, the modernization, the industrialization, of countless communities in the middle, southern and Siberian reaches of the far-flung Soviet Union. Nine-tenths of the land was never occupied or even bombed during the war. In many areas industrial and farm production doubled after 1940.

Secondly, the pre-war volume of industrial production for the whole Soviet Union was actually recovered in 1943, in several important categories. This appeared to be true in the production of all major weapons of war. Even without the Ukraine, Russia was producing more guns, tanks and airplanes than its plant was making before the war, it was officially claimed—thanks in no small measure to Lend-Lease aid from American industry.

Once conversion to peace production has been carried out, Russia may find itself right away with a higher level of industrial production than it had in 1941. Thus it is necessary to revise some earlier estimates. It seems entirely likely that the Soviet Union will, if helped by imports from the United States, surpass its pre-war production of industrial and agricultural goods round about the year 1948. When the Ukraine has come up from the depths, the nation as a whole will be the strongest single industrial power in the world, outside the United States.

Pierre Cot made the observation to me, when he was about to leave for France, that his studies had led him to the conclusion that some time between 1955 and 1960 the Soviet Union would attain a higher production level in every respect than it would have had if this war had never occurred. Barring another war, the Soviet people may by then also attain the world's highest mass living standard outside the United States.

Unfortunately, all that is not at the moment very much consolation to the war-weary men and women facing still more years of sweat, toil and rationing. Nor is it especially cheering to the Ukrainian who is paying the bigger part of the bill.

CHAPTER SIX

Verdict on Germany

I

Soviet Demands

BECAUSE Soviet policy is often first defined publicly in the form of action, some people speak about it as the "Russian enigma." And an ability to veer and tack with dramatic suddenness is indeed an important asset in Soviet diplomacy which is likely to continue to surprise us in the future. Yet there are ways to anticipate events and policy in that country as anywhere else. And in the case of Germany in particular there was perhaps less reason for mystification than seemed widely thought abroad. The central fact was obvious enough. The Kremlin did not mean to kill Germany as a state and a people, but it was determined to exterminate "Prussianism and Nazism." The problem was to find out what Russians meant by those two words.

The definition was partly supplied in a study of the *de facto* changes so speedily effected in Eastern Europe. In the summer of 1944, without people quite realizing what was happening, Moscow became the "peace capital" of the world. While the public ear in Britain and America focused on places like Bretton Woods and Dumbarton Oaks, much of the real foundation of post-war Europe was laid down in Moscow, when a whole new design for living was imposed on the defeated states.

Armistice discussions in Moscow were extremely practical affairs conducted with record speed and minimum fanfare. In a few swift weeks terms were worked out across Soviet conference tables which recognized the Liberation Committee as the ruling power in Poland, pulled Finland out of the war, set up an administrative authority to take over Czechoslovakian territory recovered by the Red Army, converted Rumania and Bulgaria from enemy belligerents into allies fighting for the Russians' cause and prepared the terms for a future anti-Hitlerite regime in Hungary.

By the end of October, after Churchill's visit to Moscow, the most important point affecting the destiny of Eastern Europe had already been decided—virtually everything, in fact, but the fate of Germany itself. The latter, too, had been worked out in the Kremlin, but censorship pressed down a severe hand on the reporting of such plans, although in Moscow the principal aims were discussed fairly candidly. In November I was finally allowed to suggest, in a dispatch sent over the Soviet wireless, the following probable Kremlin demands:

1) complete disarming of the Germany army, air force and fleet;

2) surrender of all military property to the Allies;

3) complete demilitarization of Germany;

4) complete destruction of all Nazi institutions and organizations and punishment of all German war criminals;

5) dismantling or destruction of all German war-making industry, and part payment of reparations to Russia in the form of capital goods and machinery, German aircraft, naval vessels and merchant marine, and the rolling stock of German railways;

6) use of German war prisoners as labor battalions to rebuild Russian cities;

7) cession of parts of Silesia and Brandenburg, as far west as the Niesse and Oder Rivers, and the port of Stettin, as well as all East Prussia, to the new Polish State.

I felt rather pleased, after numerous efforts, at having succeeded in getting such a speculation past Soviet censorship. I was especially interested to note that the Russians did not delete from my dispatch the following candid appraisal* of plans for Poland:

* *Saturday Evening Post*, Dec. 2, 1944.

A point to be made here is that the separation of East Prussia and Silesia from Germany may begin right away, under Red Army occupation. The Polish Liberation Committee has already issued a decree which authorizes the confiscation of large estates in lands taken back from the Reich, and their redistribution among Polish peasants. Under the Polish-Soviet agreement, providing for an exchange of populations, several million Poles are to . . . be settled in areas the Polish authorities expect to acquire from Germany.

No comparable development seems likely to occur in the southwestern zone of Germany under American occupation, nor in the northwestern area under British forces. General Eisenhower's proclamation in no way indicated support for any peasant groups demanding division of estates. *Thus, in the very beginning, there will probably be a somewhat different economic basis established for political administration in the three zones of occupation.*

Three months later, when Roosevelt, Churchill and Stalin met in the former palace of Tsar Nicholas II, in the beautiful Black Sea resort of Yalta, every one of the foregoing Russian demands was covered by the communiqué describing the agreement reached on Germany—with only two exceptions. While Churchill and Roosevelt conceded Stalin's demand "that Poland must receive substantial accessions of territory in the north and west" from Germany, in obvious exchange for recognition "that the eastern frontier of Poland should follow the Curzon line," they did not go so far as to give all East Prussia and Silesia to Poland, in advance. "Final delimitation of the western frontier of Poland should . . . await the peace conference."

The second exception was that the Crimea communiqué did not specifically authorize the use of German labor battalions by Russia. But the Big Three did agree "on common policies and plans for enforcing the unconditional terms which . . . will not be made known until after the final defeat of Germany." They also promised "to take in *harmony* all measures in Germany necessary to the future peace and safety of the world." That did not guarantee *identical* action in the three spheres of occupation, however, or the enforcement in practice, of the *same* measures.

It was pertinent, therefore, to understand what "measures" Moscow had already favored in dealing with German prisoners under her control, as the guide to coming Soviet policy in "de-Hitlerizing" that part of the Reich conquered by the Red Army.

II

Russia's Prisoners

MANY Americans were probably startled and perplexed by some of the revelations in Ernest Hauser's accounts of his visits with German prisoners in our camps in France.* The thing a Russian would find most shocking, and hardest to believe, however, was summed up in Mr. Hauser's dismal conclusion:

> No one is making an effort to mold these prisoners' minds. No one is giving them anything that might even remotely be construed as propaganda—in line with the Geneva rules. . . . They are sitting it out—on the moon. When it is all over, the doors will swing open and they will be kicked back into the still-smoking ruins. They will walk back into the desert that Germany will be after the war, with dehydrated minds. . . . The mind of a defeated German looks like one of the cities which his own stupendous crime caused to be laid waste. It is, and will remain, a vacuum.

Few Germans will walk back from Russia in that condition. About their only chance of getting back is by rebuilding their mental estates while they put the bricks together again in the places they devastated. Soviet leaders suffer from none of the inhibitions, legal or political, which prevent us from decontami-

* *Saturday Evening Post,* Jan. 20, 1945.

nating the Nazi cranium. They not only busily scrub the interior of the stubborn Prussian skull, with the aid of willing German brooms, but also sponsor a reconstruction job in that windy intellectual wasteland which Hauser found among prisoners he questioned.

Our former attitude seemed to be that once an enemy soldier surrenders, he becomes a bystander, and free from personal responsibility for his past activity. The fundamental difference in the Soviet approach was that no one was exempt from participation in the war, least of all a captured enemy soldier. He must not only stop fighting for the other side, he must begin working for Soviet victory. And if he wanted his freedom back, he must fight for it—against the leaders in whose cause he originally lost it.

That is why the Soviet Government never adhered to the Geneva convention concerning treatment of prisoners of war. In its view, all anti-Soviet war is a crime, and the idea of promising considerate treatment to a criminal simply because he has been disarmed seemed preposterous. He must first repent, then give positive evidence of his remorse. This was the case not only with individuals, but with nations that surrendered also. Every satellite power of Hitler defeated by the Red Army was obliged to reverse its policies completely and absolutely.

Even if there were no Geneva convention, however, it is doubtful if we would have tried to "cure" our captives, because among ourselves we hadn't settled on the medicine or the method of administration needed. It wasn't only the German prisoners who "talked their heads off"; you only had to turn on your radio to hear how many conflicting voices here had the only real solution for Germany. We did not organize any of "our" Germans to do the re-educating; we could not agree on what the enemy should be taught; we could not even agree that he was "teachable."

In the land of the "dictatorship of the proletariat," Kremlin leaders early agreed on what they won't have in Germany, and what they want. They also decided what to do with prisoners of war, and they set up the apparatus to achieve it. Rather, they established a branch of an already existing apparatus—the NKVD—and charged it with that specific task. To work with it, the state police had the aid of some trusted German Communists. It also enlisted the co-operation of anti-Nazi German and Austrian exiles who had been living in Russia since the rise of Hitler. These were sponsored in the organization of the Free German Committee.

There were, by the spring of 1945, thought to be altogether about 1,500,000 German prisoners of war in European Russia, Siberia and Central Asia. Thousands were already at work in the Ukraine, building roads, restoring bridges, working in the fields, and cleaning up demolished cities such as Stalingrad, Kharkov and Kiev. Long before the Crimean meeting, we saw German war prisoners at work in Stalingrad helping to build a memorial to the Russian war heroes. In the neighborhood of Kiev, when I recently visted there, some 20,000 prisoners were concentrated, according to the mayor.

"In the city itself there are only about 1,500," the mayor told me. "Most of them are cleaning up the Kreschiatic—the main street. We expect more."

"How do they work?" I asked.

"Well, you have seen them. What do you think?"

"They remind me of a slow-motion picture," I answered. Those I had watched in the street would abstractedly move a scoopful of dirt or a couple of bricks, and then reluctantly turn back for more. "How is it they work so poorly? Those I saw at Stalingrad seemed satisfactory enough."

"Ours aren't much good now," acknowledged the mayor. "But they will be. We have to use German labor; you can see for yourself how serious the Ukrainian manpower shortage is. After political methods have been applied, these men will work all right. We haven't had time for it yet."

Later on, I understood what he meant by "political methods."

In Kiev, also, I visited the ruins of a big machine works with the vice-mayor, and we inspected quarters which were being prepared to house 1,000 German prisoners. The vanguard was already there, picking up debris from the rubble-strewn grounds. The factory manager told me it would take 2,500 laborers two years just to clean up and restore the buildings in this one plant.

We stopped two of the prisoners and spoke to them until the guard intervened. But we learned that they had both been captured only a month earlier, in the Carpathian Mountains. Like all captives round Kiev, these men had not been propagandized as yet, and the piecework system of reward and punishment was not being enforced. It was later that I learned of this, from men who had seen de-Hitlerized prisoners running Soviet factories.

"In Siberia now," a Russian friend of mine returned from there told me, "whole industries are operated by German prisoners, including foremen and skilled technicians. Some of them make higher pay than Soviet workers. Our workers are beginning to complain about it."

Free Germans confirmed this. They also said that a German factory worker got the same bread allowance, in accordance with work performed, as a Russian. Ordinary German prisoners near the front to whom I spoke said that they got 400 grams— .88 lb.—of bread daily, which is what a Russian housewife or a dependent gets. Those I saw in Kiev were evidently rationed cigarettes; some smoked Russian *papirosi* as they worked.

"But after a man has qualified for factory work," one Free German said, "he can earn as much as twelve hundred grams (2.6 lbs.) of bread a day. It is true, this is more than many first-class Russian workers make. The German has to exceed his norm [basic production unit] in order to earn that much, but I know of a number who are doing it."

The energetic Stakhanovite Fritz could win extra allowances of certain foods, better quarters, clothing and special privileges. Excellent workers were promised eventual freedom—the right to go home. It was stated that some of them became "real enthusiasts." And top workers were almost invariably the quickest students at the political lectures delivered to them by Free German indoctrinators.

It is claimed that there are already more than 100,000 "de-Hitlerized" prisoners in this category of trustee workers—the majority of them taken early in the war. Many have joined the anti-Nazi veterans' committee organized under the Free Germans, and are being trained for special tasks. A few have even become "re-educators" in their own right—including some Communists recently fresh from Nazi concentration camps.

In the final scraping of the manpower barrel Himmler went into the concentration camps and dragged out even political prisoners. Germans of this character were sent to the Balkan, Carpathian and later the East Prussian fronts, where they were organized in "brigades of the condemned," to do the dirtiest work in the Army. Often they were forced ahead into mine fields, to clear a path, while covered by Nazi machine guns. Sometimes they made a break for it, and a few got through. Such men made valuable propagandists in Russia.

Incidentally, some of them reported that Gestapo and SS guards were so jittery in Germany that often they went secretly to political prisoners and asked them to sign statements asserting that they had been well treated while under their care. Fear of Russian reprisals was widespread, even before the Red Army began its drive to Berlin.

"We know that the SS has made detailed plans for the Nazi Party to go underground as soon as the Red Army occupies Germany," one officer told me. "We shall need men who know personalities and methods of the Nazis in order to weed them out to the last criminal. We shall also need police, civil servants of all kinds, trustworthy technicians and, above all, teachers. One of our worst problems is going to be the destruction of the Hitler Youth organization, which has six million young Nazi fanatics in it. They and the two million party SS men are the last reserves of Hitler's power."

---·◦⟨ I ⟩◦·---

III

The "Free" Germans

SOME earlier reports published in America about the Union of German Officers in Russia, an anti-Hitlerite group including scores of generals affiliated with the Free German Committee, were misleading in several respects. There was never much evidence to suggest, for example, that the Russians intended to elevate these officers to political power. There was no hint of an intention to recreate the German General Staff as an ally of the Red Army—a fantastic rumor. What was a possibility, and remains a likelihood, is that some of these men, individually, may prove useful in the administration of Red-occupied territory, and that anyone from Lt.-Gen. Erich von Seydlitz, who has played a leading role in both the officers union and the F.G.C., to Field Marshal Friedrich von Paulus, might head an anti-Nazi force to combat guerrillas and assassins—who caused the Red Army much difficulty in Poland.

But such general officers and thousands of subordinates who signed the anti-Hitler pledge with them were the facade of the propaganda beamed at the Wehrmacht, not the brains and the life of this work. The real leadership was supplied by political refugees who first organized the German Peace Congress in Russia in 1942, and claimed extensive connections with the underground in Germany. And its best agitators came from the German and Austrian Communist Parties, both of which still have headquarters in Moscow—for abolition of the Comintern did not, of course, mean the end of national parties. Ernst

95

Fischer, head of the Austrian exiles, and Wilhelm Pieck, of the Germans, are key figures of whom we shall hear more.

Wherein lay the potency of the "decontaminating" process used by these men in backing up the Russian merit system as an inducement to work? This should be no secret, because the essentials were constantly reiterated in *Free Germany*, published in Moscow for the prisoners' reading. But while the committee and its publication were nominally open affairs, in practice it was extremely difficult to see either one. Nevertheless, by perseverance, access could be had to both, although, in the case of party members, none granted a public interview to a foreign correspondent.

Analyzing the information available, I was able to report that the Free Germans did not preach communism or socialism as such, nor democracy as we know it, but devoted their efforts to these principal aims: 1) complete discrediting of Hitler and the upper Nazi hierarchy; 2) restoration of the German soldier's hope and faith in his people; 3) convincing both officers and men that they could, after atonement for Hitler's crimes, still have a future as a sovereign nation by co-operating closely with the Soviet Union.

Ernest Hauser's report stressed the persistence of Hitler love among the prisoners we have. By way of contrast, the full exposure and debunking of the Hitler myth was the chief theme of all Free German propaganda.

It may be noted that in the different manifestoes and statements issued at various times by German generals and their subordinates in Russia, Hitler was personally blamed—together with his cohorts—for all the disaster that befell Germans arms. Those statements were quite genuine. Early in 1943, I myself heard the first German general to surrender to the Red Army at Stalingrad—Moritz von Drebber—assert that Hitler was responsible for the disaster. Virtually all the generals thenceforth adopted the same line. It is not unreasonable to suppose that such a psychological escape mechanism was welcome, when properly presented, to any German soldier seeking an explanation and renewal of faith in the Wehrmacht and in himself.

German prisoners went through a screening which divided officers from men, separated party and army SS troops, and Gestapo members from non-party men, and singled out individuals held accountable for specific atrocities, on the basis of evidence compiled by the ubiquitous War Crimes Commission, which had branches in every army division and every local soviet. The screening also covered labor aptitude.

German agitators on the Russian side had a regular series of lectures to deliver to the more promising captives. This included chapter-by-chapter refutation of *Mein Kampf;* basic information on origins of the war and analysis of the day-by-day war news; lectures on the history of Russia, the Revolution and the Red Army; and a modified Marxist explanation of causes of the war and cures for Germany.

All of which led to the logic of the Free German program, which called for: overthrow and punishment of Nazi leaders and atonement for their crimes, liberation of political prisoners, abolition of racial laws, restoration of civil liberties, abolition of National Socialist economic laws, organization of free labor and peasant unions, confiscation of the wealth of war instigators (landowners and industrialists who supported Hitler), international collaboration for peace, with emphasis on Soviet-German friendship, and eventual reconstitution of the Reichstag by a nation purged of Nazism. It will be noted that the Crimean communiqué, which promised Germans "a place for them in the comity of nations," once Nazism and militarism have been extirpated, did not destroy the validity of the foregoing program.

Free Germans said that in practice, in areas occupied by the Red Army, there would be speedy expropriation of Junkers' estates, the liquidation of cartels, monopolies and German industrialists, and the organization of peasant unions among the newly benefited landowners. Re-education of the German peo-

ple would commence at once under joint Soviet-Free German
auspices.

A difference between the German anti-war movement of 1918
and the organization I am describing is that this one was led
chiefly by older men, some now in their fifties. Many were veterans of the First World War, in fact, and this was said to make
an impression on youngsters who had never heard anything but
Hitler propaganda. In a nation which, in 1933, polled nearly
5,000,000 Communist votes and 7,000,000 Socialist votes against
Hitler, the Free Germans did not despair of enlisting numerous
allies when they returned to the Reich.

"And do you mean to say you find prisoners sincerely ready to
support such ideas?" I asked one veteran doing the preaching.

"Not all, but some. Quite a lot. I'm convinced we've won over
thousands. It's hard work to get them to listen, at first, but not so
hard now as it was, because the new arrivals find old comrades
here, already believing in us. In the beginning, they are full of
Nazi catch phrases, but we answer these and expose them with
ideas and information the younger ones have never been allowed to hear. Some of them become interested and their minds
begin to work, and gradually they see how they have been
fooled and doped all along. They get angry and begin to read
books and ask questions, and from there on the conversion is
easier."

"So you really think some might actually fight the Nazis?"

"Plenty. We could organize an anti-Nazi volunteer army right
now."

I had no way of testing such a statement, but there was certainly a strong anti-Junker and anti-capitalistic feeling among
German soldiers, which propaganda could readily exploit along
such lines. Here were new hatreds, new enemies, to replace the
old. Here was a way out for the defeated German—something to
blame besides himself. Here was a dynamic plan of action in
place of a vacuum. When you added the fact that a prisoner prepared to join the anti-fascist organizations and submit to their

discipline had some prospect of going home, the possibility of conversion sounded not implausible.

----•:I I:•----

IV

The End of German Imperialism

BUT what about the amputation of East Prussia and Silesia, which the Russians promised to the Poles? What about the loss of the Rhineland, which Stalin urged the French to take over? What about the German industries Moscow intends to move to the Ukraine? The "ten million Germans" who are to help rebuild devastated Russia?

People doing this missionary work had these answers. First, they didn't think Stalin intended to force ten to twenty million Germans to spend their lives on Russian rock piles. They didn't think he planned to condemn the entire German people to slave labor. They said that this is the "Ehrenburg line"—Ilya Ehrenburg was the most fanatical and prolific of the Soviet eye-for-eye school of publicists—and asserted that it was not the party line. Such writing was not the tough logic of Soviet Marxist thinking.*

* This chapter was written before Mr. George Alexandrov, head of the propaganda section of the Party Central Committee, publicly rebuked Ehrenburg for an article he wrote in April, 1945, suggesting that all Germans shared war guilt and must be punished, regardless of whether they were Nazis or not. Ilya Ehrenburg, wrote Alexandrov in *Pravda*, April 14, 1945, "does not express Soviet public opinion" in his thesis of the "collective guilt" of the German people, which is "not well thought out and is visibly erroneous. . . . The Soviet people have never considered as one and the same the German population and the criminal Nazi clique ruling Germany." It is significant that this official repudiation occurred at a moment when the Red Army had crossed the Oder and was mounting its final offensive for the conquest of Berlin.

It is true enough that Marxist ideology must reject the notion that the "German mind" exists as apart from class forces which shape it, or that the "German race" is biologically and congenitally incapable of human decency. It is also true that basic propaganda in Russia usually stressed the "anti-fascist" and "anti-Hitlerite" nature of the war, rather than the anti-German.

I remember seeing a big cartoon chart in a Soviet military school which showed the figures of a Red Army man and a Nazi soldier, side by side. There was little physical difference in the two figures. But above the Soviet fighter were slogans such as "racial equality," "support of all freedom-loving nations," "people's ownership of production," "international peace," "highest development of the individual," "international brotherhood," to indicate the moral equipment which made him a good soldier. The top of the Nazi trooper's skull was cut away, and inside it the contents were displayed: "false racial theories," "ignorance," "plunder of peace-loving peoples," "Germany over all," "reactionary Prusso-German militarist tyranny," "moral filth," and so on. You got from that cartoon the distinct impression that whoever drew it believed that if you emptied out the contents of that German skull and refilled it with the correct ideas, the man beneath it would not differ so much from the Soviet hero beside him.

But Free Germans expected no such experiments to be wasted on hardened Nazis. They would be publicly tried and executed, in such a way as to condemn them not only as individuals but to discredit all their false doctrines, with the widest propaganda throughout Europe. They did think that Russia would also give long-term or life sentences at hard labor to all SS men, Gestapo men, war criminals of all kinds—including capitalists who helped Hitler—and other anti-Soviet recalcitrants. But these would total no more than four, maybe five, million people.

Second, they said the soldiers took it for granted that big slices of German territory would inevitably be sacrificed because the war had been lost. As for industries and machinery, they had never owned them anyway. In time they could re-build an industry of their own. In any case, territorial and eco-nomic penalizations of Germany were no longer unilateral Soviet demands; they were to be jointly imposed by the Big Three and the Big de Gaulle.

The real question in soldiers' minds, one man told me, was who is going to run what remains of Germany? Would the Allies really let any German regime have freedom? Was there a chance for a central government? If Germany expiated her past crimes, could a united Germany—however small—recover her sover-eignty? Could anti-fascist Germans elect their own Reichstag—in five years from now, ten years?

These pro-Soviet Germans answered the soldiers in the affirm-ative. They told the prisoners that Stalin had said Russia did not mean to destroy the German state; he had said that it was "impossible to destroy Germany." He had always drawn a dis-tinction between Hitler and the German people. Russia had no interest in ruining the basis of German livelihood—contrary, they said, to rival capitalist powers—but only wanted to make sure that its economy was not used for further aggression. Meanwhile, it was up to the soldier, if he wanted a Reichstag, to labor for it now in Russia, and work for it in Germany to-morrow.

But how explain, in this anti-Prussian, anti-Junkers move-ment, the adherence of Prussian Junkers like Marshal von Paulus and other generals? How explain the open support of Count Heinrich von Einseidel, grandson of Bismarck? These men hated Himmler, who wiped out many of their comrade generals in the purge in the summer of 1944, after the attempt on Hitler's life. The sooner the war was over, they became con-vinced, the less time it would take for Germany to recover and the more hope there would be of a future. And, very important, the more chance they would have to spend their old age in Germany rather than Siberia.

It must be emphasized that many of these teachings were

contradicted by nearly all official Soviet views I heard, which were, in the main, as follows: Russia is not interested in the German working class, which has been corrupted beyond any cure. There is no hope of a united Germany until an entirely new generation of youth has grown up, uncontaminated by Nazi teachings. Prussia itself must be obliterated. The only way to do that is to partition it among its neighbors and to break up the rest of Germany into the states of pre-Bismarckian times.

Before leaving Russia, I saw a high Soviet official and told him I had been in an argument the night before about this question: does Moscow want to move German machinery out of the country into Russia or does she want to keep some of the industry intact there, near its raw materials and skilled labor, and use its products to restore Soviet industry? It might be more efficient, for example, to keep on the spot a factory such as could produce the pumps needed in the Donbas coal mines, rather than to dismantle the whole plant or to destroy it.

"We want German industry dismantled, and what can't be moved, we want destroyed," was the official's curt reply. "We won't run the risk of its being used to attack us again—by the Germans or by anybody else."

"You mean you want all German industry removed or destroyed?"

"No, not all. Maybe we'll leave twenty or twenty-five percent, but only light industries."

"Then you're not concerned with the German working class—in making it the basis of a future pro-Soviet Germany?"

"Bah! Where is the German working class? The part of it that was any good was destroyed by Hitler long ago. What we want in Germany is the destruction of its military power, and machines and men to rebuild this country."

But when you quoted such statements to Free Germans, they weren't disturbed. The candid insisted that while that might be the opinion of a few officials at the moment, the party had a longer view. It must be interested in forming an alliance with a pro-Soviet German working class, for exactly the same reasons it wants worker-peasant alliances everywhere else in Eastern Europe. Whatever happens to Germany immediately after the war, they said, there would still be fifty to sixty million Germans left in the heart of Europe. The Russians know very well that they cannot live in a political vacuum indefinitely. "If the Germans see no hope in Russia, they will then turn westward and offer themselves to reactionary anti-Soviet elements."

The truth seemed to be that Russian Communists, although profoundly skeptical of all Germans' reliability, drilled their prisoners in anti-Nazi organizations for highly practical purposes—to get them to work, to prepare some "teachables" among them to help carry out the coming purge, and to recruit some to help police Germany.

Like all European popular-front anti-fascist groups, the German pro-Soviet movement is essentially long-term political insurance to support the Kremlin's general scheme of strategic security in Europe. While the Big Three continue to work in harmony such insurance need not be fully converted into political capital. If, later, there were signs of a split, of a Western European bloc seeking German support or of a Franco-German or an Anglo-German rapprochement, or of a re-industrialization of the Ruhr and the Rhineland, it would be another matter.

Did Yalta mean the scuttling of Soviet plans for the Free Germans? Not in the sense in which some sections of our press made out. Our diplomats evidently were given assurances that Moscow would not set up an "independent" regime in Red-occupied Germany. But it was ludicrous to suggest that Stalin had thus made any sacrifice, because there was no basis for supposing that he had ever schemed to install von Paulus or any ex-Reichstag deputy in Hitler's place. On the other hand, the Germans continued to broadcast from their station in Moscow; they continued their work with prisoners. Very likely the Free German Committee, as such, will be abolished when Germany is fully occupied; but its members will pursue their labors in other organizations. They are the nucleus of a movement to reconcile the German people to Soviet victory, and it would be absurd to expect Moscow to liquidate such an asset in its political strategy.

The reason some American commentators were confused—and were rebuked by *Red Star*—was because they never understood that, from the beginning, the pro-Soviet Germans were envisaged as having a dual role. That is, they offered not only the means for an *alternative* policy in Soviet diplomacy in Europe—one of several alternatives—but also the means for giving regional effect to objectives outlined in broad statements of what is now the *main* Soviet policy. That policy is, of course, based on a general program of co-operation with the United States and Britain in organizing Russia's security, seeking economic aid, winning firm allies along her frontiers, and building reliable bastions of friendship in every land. As long as it succeeds, that policy may limit—but it cannot exclude—a role for pro-Soviet organizations in Germany.

So the Soviet delegation should have been entirely satisfied with the Yalta declaration on post-war Germany. It in no way contradicted past inscriptions of Soviet war aims. It in no manner ruled out the use of friendly Germans in an anti-Nazi administrative apparatus to enforce the Red Army's will. On the contrary, Yalta gave Three-Power sanction to a general program within which Soviet methods of "de-Hitlerizing" Germans could be legitimately applied on a broader scale.

Furthermore, it was clear that in the "de-Hitlerizing" process the Russian Communist would apply his Marxist belief about the causes of German reaction and imperialism. These taught him that Nazism was the logical outgrowth of class domination by the landowning Junkers and the reactionary German bourgeoisie, and that the remedy lay in their extermination—a fact confirmed in a little-noticed pamphlet issued in Moscow under the title "Marx and Engels on Reactionary Prussianism."*

* July, 1943.

"The task of liberating Germany from the domination of specific Prussianism can be accomplished," according to Marx and Engels, "only by the working class, the one class in Germany which, in spite of the oppressive rule of reaction, preserved its will power, its revolutionary energy," states the editor, M. B. Mitin, Director of the Marx-Engels-Lenin Institute. Referring to the failure of the November, 1918, revolution in Germany he declares:

"In this revolution the German people should have utterly uprooted the entire Prusso-German military and bureaucratic system with its reaction and despotism, should have shattered the economic and political foundations of the rule of the Prussian Junkers and of German imperialism. . . . True, this revolution inflicted a heavy blow upon the Junkers and militarists, abolished the monarchy and proclaimed a republic, but it did not touch the economic foundations of the domination of the German imperialists, the power of the financial plutocracy. It left intact the basis upon which the rule of the Junkers rested—the private ownership of large tracts of land—and retained the former bureaucratic apparatus. Krupp, Thiessen and other fomentors and protagonists of the First World War preserved their strength in the German Republic."

Prophetically this 25,000-word tirade against landlords and financial plutocrats concludes as follows:

"The wrathful words uttered by Marx and Engels against the Prussian regime of reaction and militarism, and their impassioned summons to struggle against that system of serfdom, sound like the verdict of history pronouncing the guilt of the Hitlerite regime. The defeat of the hordes of German fascist invaders will also be the defeat of German reaction."

It follows that the "defeat of German reaction" will, in so far as the Red Army is responsible, mean the "shattering of the economic and political foundations of the rule of Prussian Junkers and German imperialism"—the expropriation and disfranchisement of landlords, along with the bourgeoisie.

On the whole, therefore, the aims of Soviet policy concerning Germany had been made manifest; likewise, the measures deemed necessary to cleanse Europe of anti-Soviet forces which might provoke a third world war or utilize Russia's neighbor states as bases for an invasion. But on another vast frontier, 6,000 miles east of Moscow, the Soviet position was not yet so fully revealed. While I was in Russia I made a continuous effort to study Soviet thinking about the Far East, in order to estimate the Kremlin's idea of the essentials of security in that part of the world, too. The pages that follow contain about all I learned.

CHAPTER SEVEN

When Russia Fights Japan

◦][◦

I

"Japan, the Aggressor"

IT ANNOYED some Russian officials to be asked about their future intentions toward Japan much as it used to irritate Americans to be continually needled in Moscow with quips about the lack of a western front in Europe. Until June, 1944, we had to spend many an hour patiently explaining the logistics of an invasion of France, and giving reassurances to agitated Soviet citizens that there would be one. Now, it seemed our turn to ask "When?"

In 1943 I wrote an article* about the sixty-four-dollar question, "Will Russia Fight Japan?", from which I want to recall a couple of paragraphs. Not because there was anything profound about them, but because they offer a basis for judgment of the influence of time on Soviet attitudes. To wit:

> The inescapable fact is that Russia cannot remain a passive spectator while alien powers enter a region of such vital importance to her, to fill the vacuum left by the defeat of Japan. For that reason, if for no other, Russia is destined to play a dynamic role in the Pacific war. But the issues and hour are as yet far from pregnant. . . . Meanwhile, three things are virtually certain:
>
> First, Russia will not voluntarily go to war with Japan until she has finally disposed of Germany. Second, Soviet diplomacy will make maximum use of the bargaining value of its strategic position in the Far East, when pressing home its case at Allied conference tables after the downfall of Hitler. Third, not till the

* *Saturday Evening Post*, Oct. 9, 1943.

moment when she can do so with least possible risk commensu-
rate with the great aims at stake, not till Japan is nearing collapse,
will the Soviet Government call upon its people to intervene in
a decisive way. Finally, when that intervention comes, it may not
conform to any preconceived patterns imagined for it.

So far so good—or bad, depending on the moral you want to
draw. Here I am not drawing anything but a picture of things
as they are and may be. Early in 1945 you could still place the
foregoing items of policy as virtually immutable, although time
had now made it possible to modify the wording of their definition. But something new had been added, and this explained
why you could talk about Russia's coming participation in the
Eastern war far more concretely and more certainly than in 1943.

I had not been back long with the Russians in 1944 before I
noticed one of those straws in the wind. We were in Rumania
with some Red Army officers and among us was a Chinese correspondent, Hu Tsi-pang. The Russians wanted to hear some
Chinese spoken; so she offered a toast, and insisted that I trans-
late it, and maybe because of that she made it a little rash. It
ended about as follows:

"Now that final defeat of Hitler is not far off, the people of
China expect that the Red Army will soon join us in destroying
the Japanese fascists, and take part in the victorious end of the
war in the East."

It may seem an innocent thing, but on such occasions a Bolshevik does not answer a toast that his Government might frown
upon. The last time I had heard an attempt like Miss Hu's was
when we were with Marshal Malinovsky, on the Don. He had
skillfully met the "crisis" with a response that gracefully converted the would-be anti-Japanese toast into just another accla-
mation for Stalin, in the text of which all mention of Japan was
lost. So now I waited apprehensively. All the officers present
looked perfectly composed. Standing up, they bowed to Miss Hu
and enthusiastically drained their glasses to the bottom.

Not long afterward the correspondents were with the Red

Army at Minsk, where they—yes, the correspondents—managed
to "capture" a few bewildered Germans. In this optimistic atmosphere someone remarked to the Russian colonel that it looked
as if he would be going home to his family very soon.

"The war is nearly over; Hitler is about finished."

"This war may be about over," replied the colonel, "but I
won't be going home just yet. We still have a score to settle with
Japan."

Little incidents like this increased after Churchill came to
Moscow in October, 1944, when it was known he discussed the
Pacific war with Stalin. And after the Chief Marshal's own speech
in November, when he branded Japan an aggressor against the
United States and Britain, Russians were somewhat less re-
strained in their comment.

"Japan, as the aggressive nation," said Stalin, "proved to be
better prepared than Britain and the United States of America,
which pursued a policy of peace." He then advocated "complete
disarmament of the aggressive nations" and the maintenance of
international security organizations. "The alliance of the USSR,
Great Britain, and the United States, is founded on vital and
lasting interests," he concluded, and *"the fighting alliance will
stand the strain of the concluding phase of the war."*

I did not know whether Stalin made any specific commitments
about the Far East during Churchill's visit—nor at Yalta later,
for that matter. What we all knew was simply that the Prime
Minister told him about the plans for a Pacific offensive which
he and Roosevelt had discussed at Quebec. But Russians used to
reading between the lines thought that Stalin's speech referred
to the whole war, and not just the European phase. The more
candid conceded it meant that Russia would be in on the "kill"
in the Far East, one way or another.

II

Psychological Preparation

CONCRETELY, the Russians had begun helping us in little ways which cannot be discussed here, but are probably well known to the Japanese. They had not turned over any Siberian air bases to us, and that wasn't likely to happen in the immediate future, but the American Military Mission in Moscow was not just sitting there thumb-twiddling. It was no secret that one of the by-products of the successful operation of three American bomber bases in the Ukraine was the organization and training of American personnel capable of operating in liaison with the Red Air Force and in co-ordination with Russian ground troops.

Even the disastrous German raid on one of our bases, to which the Soviet forces failed to assign adequate protection, was chalked up to "useful experience" by determined optimists in our Mission. "The good thing about it is that by tactful handling of the incident," one of our officers said to me afterward, "we have made sure that the Russians will not let it happen again, and we have got closer co-operation than we ever had before."

At the air bases our technicians worked with Russian mechanics and exchanged facilities and know-how. In Moscow the 100 officers and men in the Mission learned something about the country, the people, the language, and the Red Army staff, and among them were Far Eastern experts. All this, including the air bases, wasn't as important militarily as its ultimate political value could be. If Russia came in on our side, at least we would have some personnel able to work with the Red Army, which

110

was more than could be said when Pearl Harbor threw us into the "fighting alliance" against Hitler.

Meanwhile, dozens of new airfields were built in the East. The new railway from Soviet Harbor to Vitim, north of Lake Baikal, neared completion. Far Eastern industry has greatly expanded during the war and is now said to be self-sufficient in many categories. Recently I was told that the entire production of defense materials of a certain type is now being kept in the Far East. When Vice-President Wallace was in Komsomolsk in 1944 the Russians showed him a new cruiser avowedly built in the shipyards there which we didn't know existed. The Russians constantly increased their submarine fleet in these waters also.

Once I spoke to a scientist who had been in the Russian remote East during most of the war. He gave me this opinion of the feeling of people there about Japan:

"They take it for granted that we will eventually come into the war. Why? Because in its last phase, when it reaches the mainland of Northeastern Asia, it will affect our vital interests. People out there feel that the war in the Pacific concerns them more closely than the war in Europe—just like your people in California—and they are more anti-Japanese than they are anti-German. They are also more anti-Japanese than they are pro-American."

I asked him to elucidate the last point. "We have some old grievances against Japan," he said quite frankly, "but we have no special reason for wanting the Americans to move into Japan's shoes."

Russia's "old grievances" were numerous enough. They went back to the humiliating defeat of the Tsar's forces in the war of 1905, when Japan compelled Russia to give up the southern half of the island of Sakhalin, to abandon her special position in Korea, and to retire from Southern Manchuria—which marked the beginning of Japan's march down the continent. And the Bolsheviks inherited Tsarist Russian hatreds when they had to fight a bitter and savage war against Japanese interventionists.

Relations were subsequently exacerbated by Japan's seizure of Manchuria and her forced liquidation of remaining Soviet economic interests in its Northern provinces.

Japan's adherence to the "anti-Comintern pact" was italicized by further provocative actions against Russia before 1939. These included frequent attacks on the Soviet borders, and two small-scale but full-dress undeclared wars. After the Japanese-Russian neutrality pact was signed in 1941 such incidents virtually ceased, but until the Red Army victory at Stalingrad the danger of a Japanese invasion of Siberia was ever-present.

Official Moscow press comment emphasized that the Kremlin felt no special gratitude toward Japan for "refraining" from helping herself to Siberia. There were frequent reminders that the Russians fully understood Japan's hostile plans, if Hitler had taken Moscow. They would not forget the aid Japan rendered the Nazis by obliging Stalin to divert a half million sorely needed Red troops to the task of guarding Siberia.

Increased interest in hostilities in Asia, as demonstrated in the Soviet press, was considered symptomatic. For over two years, after the German invasion, the Eastern war received but briefest mention. But throughout 1944 there was a growing flow of news and comment in both daily papers and periodicals, and all of it was bad news for Japan. Long and serious accounts of sea battles were published. The landing in Leyte was thoroughly covered—which reminds me of an incident.

Japanese correspondents and military attachés, believing their own propaganda, had a big party in the Metropole to celebrate their "great naval victory" in the Philippines. While they were still drunk, the Soviet press published full accounts of Japan's defeat, based entirely on American reports. The Japanese living next door to me didn't put his head out of the door for three days. "Victory hangover," was my Russian maid's laconic comment.

Last year, for the first time, there were public lectures on Japan, and Communists included the Far Eastern war in their weekly "political education" talks to factory workers. Articles by Russians returned from Japan described the poverty and weakness of the country, and some American movies of the war were presented. A few books began to appear. In Russian naval academies the cadets began studying the campaigns in the Pacific.

Straw-seekers found a lot to interest them in Stepanov's new novel, too, called *Port Arthur*. It purports to be a historically accurate account of the first Russo-Japanese war, and it is replete with accounts of Japanese atrocities and deceit. In former days it was fashionable to dismiss this as an imperialist war, but in *Port Arthur* it becomes a patriotic war. Its heroes are the Russian common soldiers, and one or two Tsarist generals and admirals who were not, like the majority, corrupt and traitorous.

Perhaps the most significant passage in Stepanov's book is the moving speech by General Kodratenko made to his troops before the siege of Port Arthur. Kodratenko is described as a true hero coming from the masses, but in the best tradition of Kutuzov and Suvorov. He tells his soldiers that they have little hope of relief but must nevertheless prepare "to die to justify the trust of the Tsar and worthily uphold the glory of Russian arms in the Far East." Port Arthur is "Russian soil," he says, and a Russian town built up by millions of rubles "of the people's money and labor."

This book was calculated to arouse hatred of the Japanese, and desire for revenge. Opening up of old wounds in such a way at this particular moment could not bring much comfort to our "friends" the Nips. No book is published in Russia without the approval of the Communist Party, and in war-time no book appears without a political aim. A tome of over 700 pages, *Port Arthur* was published in a large edition despite the shortage of paper—heretofore reserved almost entirely for books useful in promoting the war effort against Hitler.

Diplomatically, Russo-Japanese relations grew no warmer. The Japanese Ambassador had not been received by Stalin since the war began, and nowadays Japanese were not even invited to diplomatic functions. In 1943 they still showed up at Molotov's November party, but the next year we saw no sign of them.

III

Soviet Needs in Asia

NONE of that pointed to inevitable war, but it strongly suggested ideological preparation for it. Moscow would have little difficulty finding a *casus belli* if one were needed, without leaning upon any sympathies for us. It would be natural for Red Army officers to wish to erase the long list of humiliations inflicted on Russia, and to raise their prestige still higher. Besides that, there are certain objectives Russia needs in the Far East, which the high command must regard as essential to its scheme of two-front post-war security.

Red Navy officers have made it clear that they expect Southern Sakhalin to be returned to Russia, in accordance with the Cairo Agreement, in which Churchill and Roosevelt promised to expel Japan from "all territories she has taken by violence and greed." If Moscow insists on controlling the oil of Northern Iran, clearly it would look askance at any other power seizing the oil resources of Japanese Karafuto, the only wells of importance in Northeastern Asia.

It is worth noting here that it was from Russia, not from China (which had already leased the territory to the Tsar), that Japan "took by violence" Port Arthur and Dairen. Moscow had served no notice of any desire to recover that which General Kodratenko called "Russian soil," but it probably expects to be consulted about its future, at least. As for all Japan's special rights in waters adjacent to the Soviet coastline, including fishing rights, it is assumed that these vestiges of the Russo-Japanese war will be liquidated. No doubt the Russians also intend to see that all fortifications on the Manchu-Korean borders (like those on the Polish-Czech-Rumanian frontiers) are demolished, and all naval bases in the Japan Sea and the Sea of Okhotsk are dismantled.

Another important Soviet war aim was seldom noticed in comment here. That is: to clear a way to the Pacific by controlling or demilitarizing the Kurile Islands, which lock in Sakhalin and dominate access to the whole eastern seaboard of the Soviet Union.

"We certainly won't put up with a continuation of the present situation after this war," I was told emphatically by a Russian officer back from Petropavlask, on the Kamchatka peninsula. "All our ships going round Cape Lopatka are within range of Japanese guns on Paramushiri and Kushmir, and they also have to worry about American bombers based in the Aleutians. I must say, your bombers are very accurate but they aren't too careful about their targets. It's becoming a common thing now for you to sink our ships there, thinking they are Japs. Often you don't even apologize!"

Probably the Kuriles, or at least the northernmost islands, will be considered Japanese territory "taken by greed." Japanese possession of them was recognized by Russia in 1875 in exchange for withdrawal of Japanese claims to Sakhalin. The Tsar would have taken them back if he had won the war of 1905—one reason why Teddy Roosevelt tended to support Japan. But whether Russia is awarded them now or not, the Kremlin would view with alarm the establishment of American air or naval bases to replace the Nipponese on the Kuriles.

Such were some of the conditions—there were other developments which cannot conveniently be discussed here—that led some of our best-informed Americans in Russia to talk about "when" Russia fights Japan, rather than "if." It should be

stressed, however, that these same people admitted there was
no possibility of any big Soviet move in the East till after the
end of Europe's cataclysm, and that political relations then sub-
sisting among the Big Three—and the Little Fourth—would determine the nature and the timing of Russian intervention.

Experts thought that even if the European scene permitted
Russia to start preparing immediately after Berlin is taken, it
would require some six to eight months to "ready" Siberian air
fields and move an army of millions into the East. As Hitler
collapsed in the late spring, that meant Russian action on the
other side about the end of 1945.

Russia needed to be in no sweat to rush in. Everything favored
waiting as long as possible. For one thing, her people wanted an
interval of rest and a good deep breath of peace. A short brilliant
campaign in Manchuria and Mongolia might be popular enough
if it were inexpensively won, and for demonstratively important
strategic aims. But any prolonged affair involving further heavy
loss of life would certainly sour in the Soviet citizen's mouth—at
least in European Russia.

By the middle of 1945, however, Japan had virtually no merchant fleet nor naval fleet left. She had no air force of serious
importance. What manpower she dared commit away from
home shores was fully occupied in trying to save her positions
in China, against Allied forces which would soon be carrying
out major operations there. Without a fleet and a means of sea
supply, Japanese troops in China were entirely dependent on
Manchurian war industry, which we would be bombing with
increasing severity. Japan's home front was in no position to re-
inforce Manchuria or Korea, but was calling for aid from them
instead.

Steps toward War

AGAINST such a prospect, Russia would not enter the war precipitately. She might never formally declare war on Japan at all. The Soviet role in the overthrow of Japanese fascism more likely would begin by gradually expanding aid to China. Obvious stages would be: 1) an increased supply of trucks, tanks and planes sent in by way of Sinkiang; 2) the assignment of Soviet military missions, and divisions of volunteers—Russia's whole force might be confined to an army of volunteers—to aid Chinese troops in North China and Inner Mongolia; 3) extension of facilities for trans-shipment of American military supplies across Russia to west China; 4) direct support of Chinese guerrilla troops under the Eighth Route Army in Northern China, and eventually in Manchuria, where such troops would rapidly infiltrate in advance of Chiang Kai-shek's army, as Japan's continental forces weakened. All this would be consistent with Russia's announced policy of "aiding victims of aggression."

Of course Japan might at some point, in desperation, declare war against Russia. But her moves suggested another design. One reason why Japan did not, until 1944, commit a big army to South China, to seize our airfields and complete her overland supply line to Southeastern Asia, was because she was still contemplating an invasion of Siberia. When she finally moved southward it amounted to final renunciation of hostile intentions toward Russia.

Japan could now support her armies in South China only from

Manchurian bases, and she could not support them at all if she
had to fight Russia. When Japanese war lords took this move,
therefore, they probably resigned themselves to an ultimate
complete appeasement policy toward the Soviet power. If Russia
later on demanded Sakhalin, or cancellation of fishing rights,
or the Kuriles—probably anything short of withdrawal from
South Manchuria—Japan would yield to her. Tokyo might even
offer these concessions voluntarily, though it was doubtful if
that much political wisdom would prevail.

Even if Japan did finally throw herself on Russia's mercy,
however, it would not necessarily save her, as the Emperor
could note from the case history of Bulgaria. The Bulgars were
allied with Hitler and at war with Britain and the United States,
but they still maintained diplomatic relations with Soviet Russia
up to the moment Red troops touched the Bulgarian frontier.
While we were holding armistice conversations with the Bulgars,
Moscow suddenly charged that Sofia had refused permission to
let Soviet trade representatives reside on the Black Sea, and had
been aiding and comforting Nazi troops—which was perfectly
true. The Kremlin made a series of demands, and then in a few
days broke relations and declared war. Red troops occupied
the country and eventually recognized a new government which
declared war against Germany!

All of which, from my personal point of view, was a happy
chain of events. The Metropole Hotel threw out the former Bulgarian Ambassador and I inherited his room and piano—and
his Japanese neighbor.

That Russia was, in fact, preparing to repeat some such performance, seemed obvious to many, when in April, 1945, the
Kremlin finally denounced its "neutrality pact" with the island
empire. In a terse, unfriendly note the Soviet Foreign Office
informed the Japanese Government that conditions under which
the pact was originally signed had "radically altered." Germany,
Japan's ally, had attacked Soviet Russia, and Japan had given
her aid. More important, it was emphasized that Japan had gone

to war against the Soviet Union's own allies. The pact still had another year to run—till April, 1946—but Russia expressed her contempt for both Japan's dwindling military might and for her aggressive aims, by giving this advance notice that her sympathies, and ultimately the weight of all her power, would be on the side of the Allies.

Thus it now became possible for us to discuss joint plans for Asia with Russia—a fact which naturally meant adjustment of many of our own strategic and political concepts for that part of the world. For Russia's entry into the war in the East carried many of the same implications of changed power relationships there which Soviet victory over Hitlerism brought to Europe.

There was a lot of lazy thinking by Americans before the Red Army began driving back into Europe, and consequently a lot of people were "disillusioned" to find that the Kremlin had its own ideas about how to make friends and influence people in neighboring states. Some people were going to be still more hurt —particularly those who had been shouting loudest for Russian help against Japan—when they woke up to realize that Soviet intervention against Japan inevitably would mean Soviet intervention in China on a scale comparable to our own. These people would probably even pretend to be shocked to find out that Moscow had some very concrete ideas of its own about the kind of good-neighbor it wanted in China.

Yet there was no mystery about Russia's preferences in China, not as much as there was about our own. Even more explicitly than in the case of Poland, the Kremlin had made known where its sympathies lay, what it expected of the Chinese Government, and thus on what basis it would co-operate with us. The fact that very considerable space was devoted in the Soviet press to discussions of the Chinese war effort against Japan was further evidence that the Government was instructing its people on the basis for its future policy. We ought to be instructed by it, too.

There was no problem of foreign policy facing us more important for us to grasp firmly and without any wishful thinking than that of co-ordinating Soviet-American policies in China. This was really the only place on the globe where American vital interests were crowding in directly on Soviet frontiers. I can see nothing but trouble ahead if we do not candidly face the known facts about Russia and China. And here I am going to present them in language as plain as I can make it.

CHAPTER EIGHT

The Two Chinas

I

The Kremlin Loses Patience

In 1945 a significant strain became apparent in Sino-Soviet relations, and the Crimean Conference did nothing to alleviate it, as many had hoped it might. In general the Soviet attitude had shifted from one of formal "neutrality" in the internal quarrel between the *Kungchantang,* or Communist Party, and the *Kuomintang,* the nationalist party of the Generalissimo, to one of openly expressed repugnance for the "ruling circles" of the Kuomintang's Government at Chungking, and nearly all it represented.

For six years, from the beginning of the Japanese invasion of China in 1937, till 1943, practically no adverse comment on Chiang Kai-shek or his Government was heard in Russia. Yet deep fissures in China's two-party co-operation against Japan were already evident in 1938. It finally broke down entirely in 1939, after the Generalissimo destroyed the rear echelon of the Communist-led New Fourth Army, in its only base in unoccupied China. Subsequently Chiang Kai-shek stopped paying all the Communist partisans, and imposed a blockade against their bases in North China that still exists today. Since then Kuomintang-Communist clashes behind the Japanese lines have been continuous, at times amounting to major civil war.

Despite that early break-up of the "united front" in China, however, Moscow voiced no open criticism of Chungking. In 1939, 1940 and 1941—when our merchants were still selling war materials to Japan—the Kremlin continued to lend advisers and to send supplies to the Generalissimo, even though it was then widely known that Soviet supplies were being used by Chiang to equip troops maintaining his anti-Red blockade.

By 1943, however, Stalin had begun to reveal signs of impatience. Soviet aid practically ceased. For the first time the Soviet press published a candid account of the deterioration of Chinese war leadership, and of the internecine strife which had already been widely publicized in Britain and America. Today Moscow views the Kuomintang regime with only slightly more confidence than it ever placed in the Polish Government-in-exile.

When, for example, A. Avarin wrote, in December, 1944, in *War and the Working Class,* that "calls for reform, appeals to progressive elements of the Chungking Government to take measures to improve the situation, are cries in the desert," Chinese in Moscow knew that it reflected the Kremlin's deep dissatisfaction. Mr. Avarin leveled charges against Chungking such as these: 1) its policy is dominated by reactionary militarists and defeatists who "play the role of a kind of Mikhailovich"; 2) among the 800,000 puppet troops working for Japan, nine-tenths are former Kuomintang troops, whose generals are now "serving as Quislings"; 3) the Government tolerates "unrestrained speculation" rather than help the people to develop China's resources; 4) generals such as Ho Ying-chin (now Chiang Kai-shek's chief of staff and field commander of all his armies) insist upon diverting the best-equipped Kuomintang troops to blockade the "heroic and patriotic" Eighth Route and New Fourth (Communist) troops in North China, rather than fight the Japanese; and 5) by opposing unification of China and the formation of a coalition (Kuomintang-Communist) government, high Kuomintang officials are sabotaging the war effort.

Izvestia took note of much the same factors in long editorial comments. Quoting foreign reports, it fortified its conclusion that the November (1944) reorganization of the Chinese Government—when Chiang Kai-shek's brother-in-law, T. V. Soong, became "acting premier" to replace brother-in-law H. H. Kung —represented little improvement. It was observed with disapproval that a government spokesman had declared China's Communist Party could not be legalized until after the war.

Another discussion in the authoritative *Bolshevik* reported that "forty percent of the territory of North China had been liberated by partisans operating under the leadership of the Eighth Route Army and the Communists," who "have their own administration effecting democratic measures in political life." Meanwhile it found that "Kuomintang troops act as passive spectators, at best," in the struggle for liberation of the north, "or they even assist the enemy." Significantly, *Bolshevik* concluded that only by a Kuomintang-Communist agreement could Chungking "consolidate China's position in the international situation."

Even more notable were the prophetic words of *War and the Working Class:* "It is quite clear that collaboration, the uniting of all the forces of the Chinese people, based on democratic policy, is particularly important now, when the defeat of Hitlerite Germany is approaching... *It is now impossible to put off till tomorrow the transition from the policy of reaction to a policy of progress.*"

Chungking-Moscow diplomatic relations also noticeably cooled. Even at the time of the Moscow Conference the Russians had objected when we wanted Chiang Kai-shek's Government included in the Moscow declaration. It was only the stubborn perseverance of Cordell Hull that won that concession. He was finally permitted to call in Ambassador Foo Ping-sheng from a waiting room, where he had sat cooling his heels, only when the document was ready to be signed. Since Chungking took over Sinkiang (Turkestan) from the formerly pro-Soviet governor there in 1943, and the Kuomintang extended its blockade of the Chinese Communists to include Western Mongolia,

China had not been represented in any allied consultations held in Moscow. The Ambassador had never been received by Stalin since his arrival in 1942.

II

Conflict in China

Now, what explained this new emphasis in Soviet policy? Not just the Generalissimo's reverses in South China. Every qualified observer knew several years ago that the Japanese could move in there whenever they felt the need to complete their overland supply line to Indo-China, and to deny us the use of the air bases we were so laboriously and expensively building up. The answer should be sought elsewhere—in the fundamental changes which war has brought about in the internal balance of political forces in China itself, and in the balance of international forces in the broad world arena.

For new readers it may here be useful to define the political geography inside China itself, in its simplest terms. The dominating political truth about China is that it is partly a colonial, and in the main a semi-colonial, country. The richest and most advanced areas are in Japanese hands—except where guerrillas oppose them. But the land will soon be liberated, as a result of the destruction of Japanese naval and air power, and Japan's home bases, largely by American arms—probably helped in the final stages by Red Army liquidation of Japan's continental armies. The question arises: what kind of government will prevail in an independent China, after eight years—and in the case of Manchuria fifteen years—of colonial administration?

Reconstruction is begun on the Dnieprostroi

Tilling the soil around an abandoned German tank

The trail of the Nazis

Human incinerators in Maidanek

Liberated citizens of Lublin search for their kin

Nazi stock pile of victims' shoes

First meeting of the National Committee for Free Germany

Nazi prisoners marched through Moscow streets

Red Army parachutists on the Mongolian front

Defenders of Mongolia

Nazi destruction in the Donets Basin

Gutted buildings in the wake of the Nazi retreat

Marshal Joseph Stalin

Vyaschelav Molotov, Commissar of Foreign Affairs

M. I. Kalinin, President of the Presidium of the Supreme Soviet

A. Y. Vishinsky, Procurator of the USSR

Leaders of the Soviet Government at Lenin's tomb

Government heads on their way to a Red celebration

Stalin addresses Soviet Commissars

A. A. Andreyev
Chairman of the Communist Party
Control Commission

G. Malenkov
Vice-Chairman of the
Council of Commissars

N. Bulganin, Chairman of the Commission on Foreign Affairs of the Soviet of Nationalities

A. I. Mikoyan, Commissar of the Food Industry

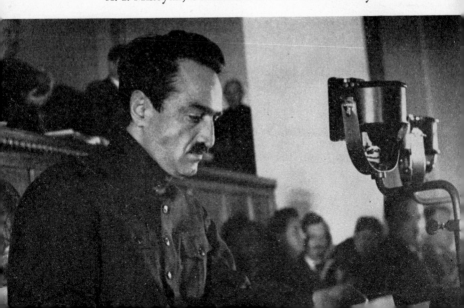

L. P. Beria,
Commissar for Internal Affairs

Commissar N. A. Voznessensky

L. M. Kaganovich,
Commissar of Heavy Industries

A. A. Zhdanov

Marshal K. E. Voroshilov

A new generation of Soviet leaders—students
of the Suvorov Military School

Church services
in the territory liberated
by the Soviet armies

Patriarch Alexei and Metropolitan
Nicolai Kurchivsky (right)

In the still uninvaded provinces of China the Kuomintang selects and appoints all officials. Chiang Kai-shek is the elected "leader" of that party and he is also the party-elected chief of the state. But not one of China's 450,000,000 people, except a minority of the 2,000,000 members of the Kuomintang, ever cast a vote to keep either that party, or its Generalissimo, in power. In this picture neither the Communists, nor any other political party, had any *de jure* existence. In fact the Kuomintang Government never officially rescinded its anti-Communist laws, which made membership in the Communist Party an offense punishable by death. Under such a regime no political opposition can exist without the support of armed forces.

But during eight years of bitter struggle against Japan the armed and politically organized following of the Chinese Communists has greatly increased. Under most adverse conditions these people have won an astonishing increment of power and territory, behind the Japanese lines, and without any help from any government—including Chungking, Moscow and Washington. Meanwhile, Kuomintang power (except that of the puppet Kuomintang at Nanking led by Chiang Kai-shek's former No. 2 man) has been obliterated in just those same areas. Hence, the ability of the "legitimate" Kuomintang to recover its power and prestige depends chiefly upon the economic, military and political support of the United States.

In the world scene, too, the picture has greatly altered. The Soviet Union is no longer an isolated and "encircled" power cautiously awaiting a trial of strength. It has won momentous victories. Now it is indisputably the strongest power, the only great military power, from the Atlantic eastward to the Pacific. Leaders in both Britain and the United States have frankly staked their future in history on making a success of keeping the peace by sharing world power with the Soviet Union. In order to do that we need Soviet agreements in Asia as well as in Europe; otherwise we shall end up in China with problems more menacing for us than Poland and Greece combined.

People who say the war hasn't accomplished anything are thus quite wrong. It has, besides destroying the Axis, and preserving our own freedom, achieved the foregoing major changes reversing power relationships. And yet that was just the thing which, in the anonymity of Moscow's polite phrase, "the ruling circles" of Chungking seemed quite unable to realize.

To understand this more concretely, one must note that Soviet policy in the East, like Soviet policy in Europe, has long been a synthesis of two considerations: a combination of supposed broad strategic needs for maximum security, on the one hand, and the skillful active promotion of political forces friendly to the Soviet Union, and likely to help improve that security, on the other. The only contradiction between these two aims lies, as we can now see, in the factor of time. In the long view the main policy and alternative policies work together; they synthesize.

Thus, Stalinist foreign policy has sometimes appeared to make temporary sacrifices in terms of distinct political aims—realization of which Communists still regard as the only true guarantee, in final analysis, of permanent peace—in order to achieve the best immediate conditions of national security. But Soviet policy is always dynamic, and on the side of political change, wherever change can help make frontiers safe for Soviet socialism.

Today, in China, contradiction between Soviet strategic needs and political aims is reduced to a minimum. It is no longer necessary for Russia to give unqualified support to unfriendly internal political forces there, purely in the interest of immediate strategic security. Future Soviet frontiers in the East, and particularly in Manchuria, can now be rendered firmly secure, provided the Japanese are succeeded by a Chinese regime backed by political forces friendly to the Soviet Union. And the international situation is now such that Russia can dynamically encourage "the transition from reaction to progress," within her general pattern of maximum security.

Another way of saying the same thing is that what Russia

wants in China, in 1945, seems to coincide with our own immediate needs. Our strategists long ago came to the conclusion, quite independent of Moscow, that unification of the military and political forces was the prerequisite of making China effective as a power against Japan and a bastion of future stability in East Asia. Obviously General Stilwell is no Communist, nor is General Hurley, and neither is taking orders from the Kremlin; yet it is now well known that both of them, as well as other spokesmen of American policy, urged in Chungking precisely the same reforms, and the same political reconciliation, as advocated by the Soviet press.

For at last it had become clear to our people that the anti-Communist groups in Chungking were not fighting quite the same war we were. From the time of Pearl Harbor onward, especially, they considered the defeat of Japan primarily our problem, while theirs was largely one of preparation for the eventual showdown with the internal opposition—the war to recover territory "lost" to the Communists, including what they had recovered from the Japanese.

"The fundamental difference between the Generalissimo and General Stilwell," wrote Brooks Atkinson in the *New York Times** after he came home with "Vinegar" Joe, "has been that the latter has been eager to fight the Japanese in China without delay, and the Generalissimo had hoped he would not have to."

One reason for Chiang's reluctance, Atkinson explained, was because "the Chinese Communists have good armies which are now fighting guerrilla warfare against the Japanese," but "the Generalissimo regards these armies (i.e., not the Japanese) as the chief threat to his supremacy. . . . For several years he has immobilized 300,000 to 500,000 Central Government troops to blockade the Communists. . . . The Generalissimo is determined to maintain his group of aging reactionaries in power until the war is over, when, it is commonly believed, he will resume his war against the Chinese Communists without distraction."

* October 31, 1944.

In 1936 the Generalissimo reportedly said, "Only when every Red soldier in China is exterminated will it be possible to talk about co-operation with Russia." Shortly afterward he was "detained" by Marshal Chang Hsueh-liang at Sian, and had to postpone his plans, but no one who knows him intimately believes that he has fundamentally changed his mind.

There was good reason to suppose that Kuomintang chieftains aimed at a strategy embracing the following steps. First, the rebuilding and modernization of Kuomintang armies, and the creation of an air force, with American help. Second, the recovery of power in the rich Yangtze Valley and Shanghai, and in Canton, behind a vanguard of American air, naval and ground forces. Third, an expedition to recover North China ports, also behind American spearheads. Finally, into Manchuria the same way.

All this the Kuomintang leaders hoped to accomplish without any serious political changes and without any agreement with, or support for, the Communist-led guerrilla forces who had spread across all the northern provinces clear to the Yellow Sea, and into the border regions of Manchuria. Chungking would first move its troops into the northern cities and onto the railways occupied by Japan. Then the Kuomintang would demand the surrender of all the partisan troops in the town and villages, as "illegal forces." Those who might resist would be blockaded and gradually exterminated as "bandits."

In fulfilling such a program, Chungking counted upon the support of American forces—right up to Manchuria and the Soviet border. Indeed, there were expressions of genuine astonishment by Kuomintang officials upon learning that Americans would like to see the two parties get together. Although General Stilwell, former Vice-President Wallace and Donald Nelson were known to have told the Generalissimo that we would not support his forces in an anti-Communist war, Chiang and his staff were reported to be still unconvinced.

III

Communism vs. Nationalism

THE basic trouble at Chungking, therefore, seemed to lie in Chiang's failure to understand the significance of the change in the internal and international balance of forces brought about by the world war. Internally, Chinese Communists have organized millions of people, with deep reserves of trained manpower, in a period when the morale and general condition of Kuomintang troops have steadily declined. Our own military observers with the Communists in North China believed that they could not be destroyed by Chiang Kai-shek's forces without American help on a major scale.

But if the Generalissimo carried out the program outlined above, very likely big forces of the Communist-led troops would infiltrate Manchuria well in advance of his own campaign. They already have nuclei there, which could be expanded on the style of Marshal Tito's forces, at a later stage, when Japan's home bases are lost. They would certainly seek unilateral contact with the Far Eastern Red Banner Army, along the extensive frontiers stretching through Manchuria and Mongolia. And if, at that time, we were backing the anti-Communist liquidation program, the Chinese followers of Mao Tse-tung and Chu Teh would probably get Red Army help, whether Russia were fighting Japan or not—just as Tito got it. That was one implication of the Soviet warnings I have quoted. In Moscow we knew that it had been reflected in informal Soviet-American diplomatic conversations.

Unless America was prepared to fight Russia then and there, the denouement of such a struggle would, I believe, be fairly certain. There would emerge a Communist-led regime in Manchuria, and quite likely a left-wing regime in Korea, enjoying Soviet backing. The Korean Communists, who are a section of the Chinese party, also have extensive connections with the Korean guerrillas in Manchuria, and would certainly rise to prominence under such conditions. Mongols in Russia told me that they expected to give eventual support to a revolt of the Southern Mongols against the Japs. There the outcome might be a re-unification of Mongolia, as an extension of the present People's Republic, under Soviet protection.

Thus, if the Communists were forced into Manchuria, we might get a regional solution of the internal Chinese struggle—but not a permanent one. Whoever rules the northeastern provinces could eventually dominate all China. Manchuria contains about ninety percent of the useful mineral and industrial resources of the whole country, and it is economically very advanced. Given a decade there, the Communists would be in a position to insist on recognition for their party south of the Great Wall, and soon we might again be called upon to preserve an anti-Red government at Nanking.

That is why the alternative seemed to be favored by us: the attempt to convince the Kuomintang that it was better to have half a loaf than none at all—more accurately, half a loaf that had been lost, rather than nothing. It was one attempt to persuade the Kuomintang to legalize an opposition and bring the Communists into a government coalition. Yet this alternative was quite as unpalatable to the Generalissimo as was the regional solution.

General Stilwell's recall was, of course, closely connected with this central question of war and politics in China. The basic trouble lay in the fact that Stilwell knew China too well. He knew the language and he knew the psychology of the war lords he was dealing with; he knew the weaknesses, as well as the potential strength, of the Chinese armies. And Stilwell knew also that in order to get Chinese troops into shape for effective fighting the command had to be separated from politics, at least for the duration of the war.

Finally, the White House and the War Department seemed to agree with Stilwell and authorized him to make three formal requests to the Generalissimo. The first called for Stilwell to be made commander-in-chief of combined Sino-American combat forces in China—with all the authority Eisenhower had in Europe. The second concerned Lend-Lease aid. Stilwell wanted complete control of this and he wanted to be able to distribute it among Chinese generals in terms of their combat potential, rather than have Chiang dole it out on a political basis. To these two requests, rather to Stilwell's surprise, the Generalissimo reluctantly agreed.

It was the third request, made in a later interview, which was the immediate cause of Stilwell's "dismissal" by Chiang Kai-shek. Stilwell himself had for some time regarded the Communist forces with respect; he had wanted to use some of their partisan leaders and troops in Burma and Thailand, but the Generalissimo had stubbornly refused. Then General Chu Teh, the Communist commander-in-chief, wrote a formal letter to General Stilwell, in which he offered to place his entire command under the American, and appealed for Lend-Lease aid against Japan. Again, on orders from Washington, General Stilwell went to the Generalissimo and asked permission to use Eighth Route and New Fourth troops in the offensive plans, and to equip them with Lend-Lease goods under American command.

Now, at this point a curious thing happened. Remember that Chiang was heavily dependent on potential American help for his recovery of power. He was in no position to refuse any reasonable request to improve the combat efficiency of China's forces. His only alternatives were: 1) to risk losing all our help, and be forced to sit on the sidelines and watch the war fought to a conclusion on other battlefields; or 2) to turn puppet and join the Japanese. Neither of these roles was a practical political possibility for him. He should, therefore, have been inclined to accept even this third request.

Instead, however, Chiang flew into a rage and staged a scene in which he was rude to Stilwell, and then sent a message to President Roosevelt asking for his recall. The explanation came out shortly afterward, according to members of Stilwell's staff. While negotiations were going on in Chungking, messages had come in to the Generalissimo from his brother-in-law and former Premier, H. H. Kung, in Washington, who was apparently in touch with somebody (the identity is still undisclosed) who informed him that, if it came to a showdown, the President would withdraw Stilwell rather than break with Chiang. So Chiang held out against placing the Communist troops on an equal footing with his own, and instead demanded Stilwell's recall—with what result is now history. Stilwell came home and General Patrick Hurley—who was also in touch with Chiang during the negotiations—became the new Ambassador and introduced a policy of appeasement of Chungking.

What the Communists were demanding was simply the withdrawal of Chiang Kai-shek's military blockade, the payment and supply of their troops with Lend-Lease materials on a basis of equality with the Kuomintang armies, modification of the one-party dictatorship, and the setting-up of a government in which they, as well as other parties, could be represented. They said they wanted a minor but a legal position, which would enable them to participate in councils and in general mobilization for an intensified war effort.

The Kuomintang, however, realized that if the legality of the party were once recognized on a constitutional basis, giving it equal privileges with the Kuomintang, it would never be possible to suppress the Communists. "After the war," Kuomintang people said, "the Communists will go on agitating and stirring up the mob to demand universal suffrage and popular elections, and we shall never get rid of them." The Kuomintang feared that they would win any mass election.

That is probably true, for these reasons. The basis of the Communist movement in China is land reform—just as it is in many countries in Europe. Since the war the Communists have stopped confiscating big estates, but everywhere they have gone they have reduced rents and taxes, "temporarily" divided the land of absentee owners, resettled landless peasants, organized marketing co-operatives, organized labor, enforced anti-usury measures, set up local self-governing councils of peasants and workers, and generally disturbed the gentry's monopoly of power.

Because they have had to build an army from nothing but popular support, and always against grave obstacles, they have learned, from seventeen years of "mobilizing the people," how to organize the peasants, how to bargain with them, what they want, and what will "work" with them and what will not. *Chiang's nationalists differ from the Communists in that they have always sought ways and means of maintaining power by keeping the peasants out of politics—they have never held a popular election in even one county—whereas the Communists perforce have had to find methods of getting the peasants actively into politics, of enlisting the mass of the people behind them, in order to sustain and strengthen themselves.*

Over eighty percent of China's population is rural. The greater part of it is hungry for land, burdened with debt, hounded by usurers, filled with hatred for grasping, corrupt high officials, and ready for a change. The working class has never had freedom of speech, press, organization or assembly. Before the war its exploitation on a sub-human standard was even worse than in Japan. It has no stake in the present regime. On the whole one cannot but agree with the Kuomintang that both peasants and workers would vote for a party which voiced their dissatisfactions—as the Communists would.

Communist Aims

FOR the foreign reader it is somewhat confusing that this Chinese agrarian-reform movement is called "Communism." In Chinese the party name is Kungchantang, which has not quite the same connotation as "Communist"; literally, it means "share-in-production party." Even if there had been no revolution in Russia there would surely have arisen some "share-production" crusade in China, with much the same aims as those of the nearly one million young people now enrolled in the Chinese Communist Party. Properly viewed in history, they are the logical successors to the many abortive peasant uprisings of the past century—bloodiest of which was the Christian-inspired Taiping Rebellion. It nearly overthrew the Manchu dynasty, and was suppressed only after the loss of about twenty million lives—with the help of the British, under General Gordon, and our own General Frederick T. Ward.

After many years of the empirical process already described, the Kungchantang is—at the moment—standing upon a moderate agrarian-reform platform, with a Marxist coloration. "Communism" in China, if by that is meant the program now enforced in areas controlled by the Communists, is a watered-down thing today. The Chinese Reds have already been through their period of "extremism." They have come to earth with many intelligent, practicable measures, fully acceptable to the peasants because they answer their immediate needs.

Communist leaders admit that it may be many years before

134

China will be able to go beyond the present "bourgeois-democratic" stage of the revolution. This stage (in their view) envisages equalization of land ownership (not collectivization); social ownership of heavy industry (railways and communications are already state-owned) and all natural resources except the land, but with a scope left for private enterprise; and constitutional government, in which all "classes" would have equal suffrage. Even under ideal conditions it would take another generation to realize that program. Theoretically, there is no reason why the Kuomintang and Kungchantang couldn't work together in a coalition government during that period.

But here a word of warning. It is wrong to suppose that these people do not aspire to ultimate complete power. It is also wrong to suppose that they, any more than the Kuomintang, would establish a liberal democracy in China in the American sense, although they would probably bring about a kind of democratic equalitarianism, such as is now realized in areas they control. China is still a semi-feudal country and has never known the luxury of capitalist democracy, as liberals know it, and probably never will in our time, whoever rules.

The whole war is regarded by both sides as a continuation of the long internal struggle for power. The Kuomintang is quite correct when it says that the Communists have "utilized" Japan's invasion in order to expand—although Communist "expansion" has occurred entirely behind the Japanese lines, no attempt having been made to invade any of Chiang Kai-shek's "own" territory in unoccupied China. But the Kuomintang has also utilized the war to hold power; in the "emergency" it has denied recognition to the Communists and other political opposition. "War is a continuation of politics" even in our country. In China, where the center of national power has never been fully stabilized, politics is the essence of war; political organization exists only as an organic part of military organization.

"We must struggle for leadership everywhere and at all times," I was told by Po Ku, a leading member of the Chinese party's

Politburo, as far back as 1938. "We do not deny that. A political party that does not lead has no reason for existence."

Thus, it is misleading to contend that Chinese Communists are not Marxists, or that they do not hope, ultimately, to build up a classless, socialist state in China, or that they are not very close to the Soviet Union in their sympathies. People who try to persuade Americans to accept them on the ground that they are not "real Communists"—in the foregoing sense—are either misinformed or deliberately dishonest. That kind of argument belongs in the same category with appeals to tolerate Soviet Russia because it is "abandoning Communism," which it obviously is not, or because it offers us a huge post-war panacea market and a solution to our unemployment problem, which it cannot.

Nevertheless, there is a very strong "nationalist" element in the Chinese party—as in Russia and among other European Communists. Mao Tse-tung was once expelled by the Comintern for "deviation," and he and Chu Teh first organized the Chinese Red Army without Russian directives, and only later won Comintern sanction. Having built up their armed power long after Moscow had more or less forsaken their struggle as hopeless, the Chinese Red leaders have a strong sense of independence. We begin to see that here, as in Europe, the coming to power of Communists will not wipe out nationalism overnight. Once a party has the responsibility of state power it tends to inherit all the national history and culture, and to cling to all the national aspirations—in a political sense—that go with it. In Russia it took the communists twenty-five years fully to recognize that fact. In China, because of their prolonged and bitter armed struggle for existence, the Communists have learned it before attaining full power.

Another thing. Whoever runs China will have to look chiefly to America for economic help. This factor is certain to influence internal and foreign policy. Russia herself would not be able to help China on the scale needed, not for some years.

On the other hand, we have already given up extraterritoriality to the Chungking Government. This means that whatever happens, the era of foreign concessions, foreign capital investment in terms of great economic monopolies, has passed. But both the Kuomintang and the Communists would expect to get large American government loans to build up the country, and to develop industry and service facilities which could, as soon as possible, be operated entirely by Chinese.

One very important observation, however. Under a Communist-dominated government there would be state planning. Industrialization of the country would probably aim primarily at the internal market—the achievement of self-sufficiency, production for use, and elevation of the people's own standard of living, as in Russia. The Communists themselves would not be bankers and industrialists, nor interested in personal profits. Under the Kuomintang, whose present rulers (the Chiang-Kung-Soong family) are the nation's richest industrialists, bankers and landowners, China would prematurely enter the world market, as did Japan, and as Indian capitalists seek to do today. There would be sharp competition for overseas trade lost by the Japanese, for the fattest profits on goods produced by cheap, coolie-level slave labor always lie in the world market. Kuomintang China had already entered the world market with such goods even before the war. Ironically enough, this central fact was not in the least understood by American labor-union leaders. Throughout the war they poured "relief" money into the hands of Kuomintang labor bosses representing the philosophy of cheap controlled labor—one of the worst menaces to the maintenance of decent wage standards for free labor in the advanced capitalist countries.

But would not our economic collaboration with a China influenced by Communists tend to comfort the cause of Communism in general? Obviously it would—though not nearly so much as our present and future aid to Soviet Russia. We face here exactly the same choice—and the same dilemma—which we have already settled in general agreement with Russia throughout Europe.

V

Can China Unite?

FINALLY, would not a Chiang Kai-shek China be more likely to support our side in some future hypothetical war against Russia? Not necessarily so—if the Kuomintang's party boss, Chen Li-fu, succeeds in building up the kind of Oriental fascist state he has been aiming at. But even as late as 1945, the anti-Communist group in Chungking probably would not have rejected such an opportunity. Which was precisely what the Russians didn't like about Chungking—and why they looked upon our promotion of the Generalissimo as one of the Big Four, or the Big Five, with distrust and suspicion. If the Dumbarton Oaks proposal is adopted, Moscow knows that we and the British could always count on Chiang for the necessary vote in any issue against Russia—just as surely as we could count on Franco's vote, if Franco had a vote. In view of the fact that China is a neighbor of the Soviet Union, while we are separated from her by a very wide and deep blue ocean, the Russians think they have a right to expect a friendly ruler and a friendly government there.

Whether, in a possible future anti-Soviet war, the Generalissimo's help would be worth more than it is now, however, or whether he would still be saving up ammunition to "resume his war against the Chinese Communists without distraction," as

Brooks Atkinson put it, is another question. In any case, if we are going to fight Russia some day, as pessimists believe, we have been backing the wrong people everywhere else, this war has no meaning, and this analysis should be "included out."

But Roosevelt's foreign policy clearly was *not* based on that assumption, and hence he went on trying to persuade the two Chinese parties to work together. In response to American pressure, however, Chiang's main gesture was to offer a *yu-ming wu-shih*—"name without reality"—formula of liberalization, in an attempt to maintain the political status quo. The Generalissimo is a maestro at this kind of maneuver. For example, after the Stilwell scandal he made a great show of "reforming" his government by removing the much-hated and reactionary Ho Ying-chin as Minister of War. But he promptly sabotaged his new war minister by appointing that same Ho commander of all his ground forces, and Chief of Staff.

Again, in a New Year address, the Generalissimo promised that a constitutional convention would be called in 1945. But the rules laid down in 1936 for the selection of delegates to this convention, which has already been postponed a half dozen times, remained unchanged. They provide for an overwhelming majority of self-appointed Kuomintang delegates and hand-picked henchmen. The time was, however, much later than the Generalissimo thought. A "democratic" convention of such a nature, which would merely confer constitutional status on his own "group of aging reactionaries," to quote Atkinson once more, could neither solve his internal dilemma nor meet conditions created by the new balance of international forces.

The late President himself saw through the speciousness of Chiang's "constitutional" plans. The last time I saw him was the day after he made his report to Congress on the Yalta Conference, and now that he has "slipped away" there is no reason why that conversation cannot be reported here. A little while earlier he had been asked, in press conference, to comment on

Chiang Kai-shek's announcement that he intended to call a "constitutional convention" in 1945. Roosevelt had pointedly avoided comment and had merely said, "That's very interesting news."

Afterward, in private conversation with me, he revealed that he was fully informed about the limitations of that convention, and of the Kuomintang's plans to pack it with their own delegates. He also showed considerable impatience with Chungking's attitude in the negotiations which had been dragging on for months, in an effort to solve the internal deadlock. He said that he had had hopes, for a while, that Hurley might be able to bring the two parties together; that a formula had been sent up to Yenan and that the Communists had made some amendments to it. "Now everything seems to have fallen down," he said, "because the Kuomintang has raised some perfectly absurd objections to the amendments of the Yenan Government."

The President asked me my opinion of Chiang Kai-shek, and then he said that he himself felt he didn't know him at all. "I wasn't able to form any opinion of him in Cairo," he told me. "When I thought about it later, all I knew was what Mme. Chiang told me about her husband and what her husband thought. She was always there and she phrased all the answers. I got to know her, but this fellow Chiang—I felt I never could break through to him at all."

Roosevelt said that he had become convinced that the Chinese Communists were in reality trying to realize an "agrarian reform" program, and not Communism. He also told me quite flatly that he was determined to "work with both Governments in China." He was anxious to see organization of guerrilla forces in North China, to aid our landings there. I had said that I supposed as long as we recognized Chungking it would be impossible to aid the Communist forces. "We can't support two Governments in China, can we?"

"Well, I've been working with two Governments there," he responded, throwing his head back emphatically, "and I intend to go on doing so until we can get them together."

That seemed to me sufficient evidence that, whatever was said about China at Yalta, there was no basis for the rumor that a deal had been made, in which the Russians had given us a "free hand" to back Chungking to the limit, in exchange for concessions we had made about Europe. It also seemed to show that the President was deeply skeptical of the promises of "constitutional government" announced from Chungking.

In any case, the Chinese Communists lost no time in disassociating themselves from the Kuomintang's plans to give its regime a constitutional aspect. The Yenan press branded the project as a potential "congress of slaves," and insisted that only an assembly chosen by the people in free elections, and by direct vote, could frame a democratic constitution. In March, also, for the first time since 1937, Yenan denounced Chiang personally as a "despot" and "dictator" and called for his removal as head of the Government. What was more interesting still, *Pravda* used the same language. As this open crossing of swords coincided with Patrick Hurley's return to this country, and close upon the convening of the San Francisco Conference, it had to be interpreted as a complete vote of non-confidence in Chungking as the legitimate government of China.

Thus the irreconcilability of the internal forces represented by the two parties seemed to be deepening, as the major threat of Japan diminished. Today, any fundamental agreement between Chiang Kai-shek and Mao Tse-tung seemed possible on one of only two conditions: 1) that the Communists surrender their armed forces to the Kuomintang, and abandon their struggle for leadership and ultimate power; or 2) that the nationalists give up their monopoly of power, grant suffrage to the people, and permit them to elect a democratic government. Neither of those conditions seemed likely to be realized.

What became obvious then was that only combined Anglo-American-Soviet pressure on both parties in China could impose a formula even temporarily uniting the anti-Japanese forces in our common war. Such a compromise might make it possible for the United States and Russia to work with the same Chinese Government, to avoid the "bolshevization" of Manchuria, and to prevent a return to the old pre-invasion system of two Chinas —one in the north and the other in the south. It seemed certain, in fact, that Roosevelt discussed China with Stalin, and explored the basis for a joint policy, when they met in the Crimea. But what Stalin said, or did not say, or refused to say, on that subject, was another one of those things the world would likely become aware of only when it was translated into action.

And here is as good a place as any to take a look at the ruler of all the Russians, the cobbler's son from Georgia, who will have as much to say about the future of Asia as he has already had to say about the destiny of Europe.

CHAPTER NINE

Stalin at War

—◦❚❘❘❘◦—

I

Russia's Hero No. 1

OF ALL the unenviable responsibilities which Harry S. Truman inherited, perhaps his most difficult task was to replace Roosevelt in the relationship which the departed Chief established with Joseph Stalin. Whatever qualifications existed in the respect and confidence built up between the two war-time mentors, it is certain that they had learned to understand and appreciate each other to a degree no one would have believed possible before 1941. Much of the hope of the civilized world rested in faith in the ability which they had demonstrated to compromise and co-operate on common problems in politics and war.

We cannot yet know whether the old personalized pattern of a Big Three will again be restored. Whatever happens, however, President Truman will be obliged to make as shrewd a study of the Soviet leader as his predecessor did, in his effort to rid the world of aggression and to stabilize world peace. The natural gulf which must separate the thinking of a Missouri-born farmer from that of a cobbler's son in Bolshevik Russia is bound to be a deep one, and in Truman's effort to hold the bridge which now unites our two nations he will need all the intelligent backing and understanding of the American people.

Here I cannot attempt any full-scale portrait of Stalin and his significance in history, past and present. Yet it may be of some value to tell something about how this man looked to people outside the Kremlin walls, while Russia was at war. It seems to

me a useful thing to do because in the Russian acceptance of
Stalin, and all he represents, you see most clearly the wide difference in political and social thinking that lies between us, and for
which we must make full allowance if we are to live together
in harmony.

Perhaps the most difficult thing to understand in Russia, for
anyone brought up in the Anglo-Saxon tradition of democracy,
are the roles which Premier Stalin plays in the party, the Government, the armed forces, and the mythology and ideology of the
nation. No other political figure in the world performs so many
varied functions, real and symbolic, and his position is something which can be fully comprehended only as a combination
of traditional Slav-Tartar Russia and the modern institutions and
instruments of Soviet Marxism.

The average Englishman or American, however objective he
may feel in his approach to Soviet Russia, is nearly always deeply
puzzled, if not actually shocked and nauseated, by the omni-
presence of the ritual of Stalinist hero-worship which he finds
there. Very often this phenomenon alone so prejudices the foreigner, particularly one who has lived only in countries with a
parliamentary tradition, that he becomes blinded to any benefits
which the Soviet system may have brought to a nation so unlike
our own in its history.

Although Marxism and the Soviet state reject idols and gods,
as well as God, there is something fairly close to a substitute for
all of them in the cult of adoration built up around Stalin. There
is Stalin the statesman, Stalin the practical politician, Stalin the
national leader, Stalin the Marxist. But apart from those and
other personalities there is this Stalin who, for the ordinary
Russian peasant or worker, or warrior, stands above and beyond
all the pettiness and limitations of office, and all the frustrations
which encompass his own life. There is Stalin the Great.

Red Army flyers are not just heroes; they are "Stalinist fal-
cons." Red Army infantrymen are armed with "Stalinist rifles"
and cavalrymen with "Stalinist sabres"; in the final offensive it

was the Stalin tank which ripped up Hitler's battered armor. In the rear it is the "Stalinist spirit" which is everywhere invoked to inspire men, women and children to bigger and better things. In athletic meets it is "Stalinist youth," singing ballads glorifying Stalin—in all languages of the Union—that marches into the stadiums under standards bearing portraits of the leader.

Every schoolroom, every public building, every factory, and nearly every home, has its statue or portrait of Joseph Vissarionovich in one of the conventional, standardized poses. During the bitter winter of 1942–43, when the big Mostorg department store had nothing on its shelves yet kept its doors open, there were always images of National Hero No. 1 for sale there. Bookstores might have nothing else, but in their windows were always displayed the works of J. V. Stalin and Lenin. The paper shortage was severe and even big dailies like *Pravda* and *Izvestia* were cut down to four pages each. Very frequently two of the four pages were devoted to portraits of Stalin, or orders of the day signed by him, and letters from him and to him from all kinds of people and all parts of the Union. Once I counted Stalin's name repeated in one day's four-page paper fifty-seven times, and this was exclusive of further reminders in the form of geographical place names like Stalingrad, Stalino, Stalinabad, etc. Week after week there appear long resolutions passed by collective farmers, factory workers, citizens of all occupations, first making promises to Stalin of the work they will do, then announcing to him that their plans have been overfulfilled.

Poems and ballads pour into the press, occupying a half page or a full page. On December 14, 1944, for example, a "poem consisting of ten cantos and a dedication to Stalin," took up a full page in all papers. It reportedly bore the signatures of 9,316,973 Ukrainians, started off, "Father, teacher and beloved friend, accept this story of the glorious fight of the Ukraine," and ended up "Glory to Stalin!"

"What is the real need for all this?" I asked a Russian Party man one day, honestly seeking enlightenment.

"Everything in this country," he answered, "is dedicated to the idea of making a success of building socialism in one country. Stalin, more than anyone else, proclaimed and enforced that policy. Experience has shown that we Russians like to have a national hero who symbolizes perfection and greatness. In the Communist view the revolution itself is the hero, but that idea is too impersonal for the masses. In a country building up socialism against great obstacles we had to have someone to personify the revolution, just as in former times the Tsar was the hero-god of Holy Russia. But the revolution, unlike the Tsar, permeates every aspect of a man's life. Therefore, as its personification, Stalin must also appear before the worker in every aspect of his life."

Now, in America and England that kind of thing would eventually boomerang. There is something in our tradition which rejects excessive glorification of any living man, however gigantic his stature; the greater he is, the more we like to hear about little weaknesses that remind us that he is, like ourselves, made of the common clay. It is only in death that we recognize greatness and give it true acclaim and reverence—as America did with so full a heart when Roosevelt left us.

Ordinarily, we instinctively understand and sympathize with that unknown democrat in ancient Athens who Plutarch tells us voted against Aristides the Just. The vote of ostracism was being taken as between Aristides and an opponent, when a citizen approached Aristides in the street. Explaining that he was illiterate, the stranger asked Aristides to inscribe a potsherd in a vote against himself. Curious, the honest old jurist asked the citizen, "Tell me, has Aristides ever done you any harm?"

"No, none whatever," was the Athenian's reply. "But I am just so *bored* with hearing him called Aristides the Just!"

The Russian peasant or worker might not appreciate that story, nor readily acknowledge a parable. I remember how repeatedly I was asked by Russians, during our last national election, why it was necessary for President Roosevelt to be subjected to all the strain and embarrassment of a campaign. Hadn't he served the country well? Was this an appropriate reward for all his sacrifice in the interest of the nation? They seemed to feel genuinely mystified by this phenomenon of a great national hero being subjected, by the generous American people, to the humiliation of an election.

Stalin, it is true, was also elected to his office, by both party and government bodies. But not for many years has there been any opponent, and the vote has always been unanimous. Today it is inconceivable that Stalin could be removed while still able to lead the state, and the mere thought of it seems hard for most Russians even to consider. I suppose a fairly typical reaction was that of a young Communist I know, when I asked him abruptly one day, "What would happen to a man who stood up in Red Square and shouted, 'Down with Stalin!' "

He hesitated for several seconds and then replied. "It just would never occur!"

"Well, but suppose it did? What would happen to him?"

"People would just stare at him in astonishment. Then a policeman would eventually come along and take him off to an insane asylum."

On the other hand it is true that Stalin has numerous individual enemies in the Soviet Union and that even to many loyal intellectuals much of the ritual is as tiresome and naive as it seems to Westerners. Yet the enthusiasm with which he is acclaimed by countless millions of less sophisticated Russians seems to be genuine. It is impossible for a foreigner to guess with anything but rough accuracy at the real feeling of the Russians, but what opposition to Stalin's personal authority as head of the state still exists is now totally unorganized.

One of the last centers of opposition to be reconciled was the Orthodox Church, whose allegiance was among Stalin's wartime triumphs. "Divinely-installed Leader of the people of our

great Union," the late Patriarch Sergeus called this Georgian
atheist. And in 1944 the new Patriarch-Elect, Alexei, warmly renewed the Church's pledge of loyalty. "Most revered and dear
Joseph Vissarionovich," wrote Alexei, "I ask you to accept these
assurances and believe in the feeling of profound love and gratitude to you with which all church workers, guided by me, are
now inspired."

The horrors of this war have tended to obscure, though not
to erase, the public memory of grievances accumulated against
the party leadership during the excesses between 1936 and
1939. Those prominent Bolsheviks who were publicly tried and
condemned very likely were guilty of the crimes to which they
freely confessed, but during the hysteria of general purges
which followed, many innocent people were pushed into exile
or worse.

The sadistic Yagoda and Yezhov, who for a time ruled a state
within a state—the Gaypayoo—were chiefly responsible for
these outrages. By Yagoda's own account his hirelings faked
thousands of documents and so mixed up the records that it
was impossible to tell a genuine dossier from a bogus one.
Curiously the public does not seem to blame Stalin for having
permitted such a Frankenstein to develop, but instead gives
him credit for having cleaned up the Yagoda gang and brought
the secret police back under full control of the Politburo—which
he did when the Gaypayoo was crushed.

Stalin then made his fellow Georgian, Lavrenti Beria, head
of the new home security troops under the NKVD. Thousands of
people—no foreigner can know how many—remain in exile and
whole factories, if not whole towns, are run by the NKVD. But
during the war many of these "involuntary workers," as Walter
Duranty likes to call them, were given a kind of amnesty, to join
the Army, and many have now been fully reinstated, some on
Stalin's personal order. An odd fact told to me by a Russian who
should know is that thousands of these exiles have voluntarily

written letters full of praise and gratitude to Stalin, thanking
him for having purged the traitors and led the nation to salvation.

In any case, Stalin is certainly not popularly thought of in
Russia now as a capricious tyrant, as some critics abroad imagine.
However it may have been in the past, no one who has lived
there during the war can doubt that in the future Stalin will be
respected as the man who led all the Russians to the greatest
military victory in their history. Nor is there much reason to suppose that tens of millions do not accept, at face value, Stalin's
own explanation of the motivation of his work:

"The task to which I have devoted my life," he said, "is to
elevate the working class. That task is, not to strengthen any
national state but to strengthen a socialist state—and that means
an international state. Everything that contributes to strengthening that state helps to strengthen the international working class.
If every step in my efforts were not directed toward strengthening and improving the position of the working class, I should
consider my life purposeless."

Stalin's genius lies first of all in his skillful manipulation of all
the forces in political life, and he is fully aware of the value of
hero-worship in enhancing his own prestige and that of the
party. Lion Feuchtwanger once asked him whether he approved
of the use of his portrait and image everywhere and he answered,
"If the people want it, I see no harm in it." To Emil Ludwig, another German author, he denied any contradiction between the
materialist conception of history and the fact that great emphasis is placed on the role of personality in the Soviet interpretation of history—in that case the role of Lenin.

"No, there is no contradiction," Stalin replied. "In *The Poverty
of Philosophy* and in other works of Marx you will find it stated
that it is people who make history. But of course people do not
make history according to their own fancy . . . they make it only
to the extent that they correctly understand the conditions they

find ready-made and to the extent that they know how to change those conditions."

Ludwig then said that in his youth he had been taught by German professors that Marxism denied the role of heroes and hero-worship in history.

Stalin: "They were vulgarizers of Marxism. Marxism never denied the role of heroes. On the contrary it admits that they play a considerable role, only with the provisos I have made."

II

Stalinia

YET despite the adulation to which he is constantly subjected, it is agreed by men who have had contact with him, and it is obvious from his works, that Stalin is no neurotic megalomaniac. Throughout the war he has maintained an active sense of proportion and a Russian sense of modesty. Stalin has never made any claims to supernatural guidance or claimed messianic wisdom, nor does he affect the personal mannerisms of a dictator. It cannot be shown anywhere that he ever boasted of adding any new principle to Marxism, though he has not opposed the use of the phrase Marxism-Leninism-Stalinism.

"I am merely a pupil of Lenin," he likes to repeat, "and my aim is to be a worthy pupil of his." An odd but perhaps significant point: the highest peak in the Soviet Union, in the Pamirs, is called Mt. Lenin; the second highest, Mt. Stalin.

Appreciation of the limitations of his own knowledge evidently saved Stalin from interfering disastrously with the work of experts. He never made the mistake of setting up headquarters at the front, and countermanding tactical plans, as Hitler did. And there are many indications that he interests himself especially in scientists and research workers, whom he apparently does not attempt to lecture about their specialties.

A typical story which gives an insight into Stalin's success with scientific men was told by S. Lavochkin, a young Soviet aircraft designer. Stalin had called him in and demanded that he redesign his craft to increase its cruising range. Lavochkin replied that, quite frankly, it was impossible to do so without sacrificing some more important virtues of the plane.

"Think it over," said Stalin, and walked away. When he returned Lavochkin gave him the same negative reply. The young man must have been shaking in his shoes—when to his relief Stalin smiled and said, "What can I do with you? Well, let's leave it as it is."

During Churchill's visit to Moscow in October, 1944, a special performance of the French ballet, *Giselle,* was given in his honor at the Bolshoi Theater. Stalin unexpectedly appeared in the box for his first public visit to the Bolshoi since the war. But when, during intermission, the audience rose in ovation, he retired in order to let Churchill take the applause; and he only returned when the British Premier went out and fetched him. Then, however, he joined in with the applause in his own honor—an old Russian custom, apparently. Stalin clapped, too, when the Red Army band played the Stalin Cantata, while Churchill turned away rather impatiently, and kept his hands folded on his knees.

It was very interesting to watch the two great men together that evening, side by side. Standing up, Stalin was slightly shorter than Churchill, who is about five feet six. There was still a certain pantherish grace and quickness of movement in the rotund Winston; Stalin moved slowly, almost augustly. Churchill's mobile face and bodily movements frequently betrayed his reaction to the stage or to something said by a guest in the former Imperial Box, which he occupied. Stalin remained almost motionless and expressionless throughout the performance. Once or twice Winston half turned, as if about to make an apt phrase or epigram to Stalin, but checked himself, apparently realizing that his subtle command of English would be lost in the translation.

Only once did Stalin show any marked emotion. It was when a famous Russian baritone, Razumovski, sang the nostalgic Russian folk song, "Glorious Sea, Holy Baikal," which tells of the lonely suffering of exiles on the Siberian steppe—where Stalin spent some years as a political prisoner. Stalin pulled out a large brown handkerchief, wiped his eyes, and vigorously blew his nose.

Only a man of immense patience and endurance could follow Stalin's routine. He usually spends the afternoon at his desk in the Kremlin and then works all night. Very often he is host at Kremlin banquets, where the procedure follows a monotonous pattern, beginning with two or three hours of dining and wining, succeeded by entertainment of some kind, usually a movie, which lasts till midnight or later. Stalin drinks ten to twenty toasts, but usually in red wine only. At sixty-six his health is still good and he apparently has no serious ailment, but his hair and the famous mustache are now totally gray. Habitually he follows up one of the late Kremlin parties with four or five hours of hard work.

Around Moscow there are nearly always distinguished foreigners, or delegates from various remote parts of the Union, waiting to see the Premier. His schedule is made up far in advance, by his numerous secretaries, and frequently people wait weeks to see him. In the winter of 1942–43 we saw a delegation of more than a score of Mongolians, led by their Premier, hang around the Metropole Hotel for six weeks until Stalin could fit in a banquet for them. One of our American Air Forces generals sat in Moscow for two months, waiting to discuss business with Stalin, on a mission for General Marshall. Maj.-Gen. Patrick Hurley, armed with a letter from the President, was also left stewing for a fortnight before he crashed the Kremlin gates. Yet Stalin frequently broke his schedule to see an unknown peasant or worker who had distinguished himself in some way, or to congratulate a Red Army hero.

During about a year spent in the Soviet Union, in which I attended several state functions, I saw the Soviet Premier at close quarters only once. Throughout the war no foreign correspondent interviewed him, though on several occasions he answered their letters—the most celebrated case being his brief messages about the second front to Henry Cassidy of the *Associated Press*, which were major scoops. Alaric Jacob, of the London *Daily Press*, was the only correspondent who got near enough to him to exchange personal greetings—but didn't. Thereby hangs a tale.

When Churchill invited Stalin to dine at the British Embassy, during his visit in October, 1944, Sir Archibald Clark-Kerr consented, as a special concession, to let one correspondent stand just inside the door, to watch the great man arrive. Jacob was our delegate. It happened that Stalin was nearly a quarter of an hour late, a rare thing, and as a result everyone had drifted away from the foyer to find out what was the matter; a hitch was suspected and telephone inquiries were being made. Suddenly Stalin opened the door and walked in, alone. Jacob was the only man there and Stalin removed his marshal's hat and made the gesture of handing it to him. There was a tense moment of conflict between Jacob the public-school boy and Jacob the journalist, but the former won out. He declined to serve as footman, turned his head, and thereby missed being the story of the week. The odd thing about it is that Jacob is among the very best British correspondents in the business.

Often host himself, Stalin is seldom a guest. The psychological and strategic advantages of being host had an influence at both Teheran and Yalta. Stalin's visit to the British Embassy therefore broke all precedent. It was the first time he had set foot in a foreign embassy in his life. As a precaution, the NKVD sent a detachment of white-clad special guards, who took up positions at various points throughout the old mansion, which stands on the Moscow River, just across from the Kremlin. When Churchill's Scotland Yard men, who were also along as bodyguards, saw Stalin's men disposing themselves around the place, they were much disturbed.

The captain finally went up to Churchill and said, "Your Honor, I don't like the looks of this, these foreign troops on His Majesty's soil. It's highly irregular, sir."

Churchill looked at him gravely and nodded agreement. "I'm afraid we'll have to put up with it, though," he replied, "just this once."

Stalin's visit to the British Embassy did not, however, break his routine of all-night work. He kept Churchill, Eden, Clark-Kerr, Harriman and the rest of the guests up all night, talking mostly about the Poles and what could be done with (and/or to or for) them.

In summertime one of Stalin's cars (usually a Packard) may be seen speeding out of the Kremlin gates at about dawn, when the marshal goes to his country estate, in the old Tsarist palace outside Moscow. In winter he usually lives in the Kremlin, in what has been described, by Russians who have seen it, as a modest six-room apartment. No foreigner has, to my knowledge, ever been inside Stalin's Kremlin home.

Stalin's personal life is rarely discussed by Russians and never in the press. His one daughter, Svetlana, an attractive girl of eighteen, is perhaps closer to him than anyone else. She went to a public school near the Kremlin and was much liked by her fellow students, I was told by one of them. She took part in all the school activities and was treated much the same as anyone else. In 1944 Svetlana was married, but there was no mention of it in the Soviet press and it took correspondents days to find out the name of the bridegroom.

Stalin also has two sons, who were both in the Red Army. Vassili, the elder, by Stalin's first wife (whom he divorced), fell into the hands of the Nazis early in the war and Goebbels offered him great inducements to denounce his father. He never did so; at

this writing his fate is still unknown. The other son, Jacob, by
Stalin's second wife, was carefully watched over by his superiors
and seldom succeeded in getting to the front. He could often be
seen around Moscow. It seems strange, but the average Russian
does not know whether Stalin himself ever married again, after
the death of his second wife. Some say yes and some say no. His
few intimate associates who really have the answer would never
discuss the matter with a foreigner.

III

That Man in the Kremlin

IT IS widely supposed abroad that Stalin is a poorly educated
and uncultured man, a notion fostered especially by Trotsky and
his followers. The fact is that he graduated from an Orthodox
school in Georgia, where he was born, and then attended an Orthodox seminary. He studied to be a priest till he was twenty,
when he was expelled for revolutionary activity. No doubt many
of his Jesuitical traits trace to that early religious training. But
during the last five years of his seminary days he was already
deep in Marxism, an enterprise in which he later had a distinguished teacher, Vladimir Lenin. Though he thus had a nar-
row doctrinaire education, he obviously overcame its handicaps
sufficiently to deal with the many complex phenomena of Russian
society—on the understanding of which his leadership was
consolidated.

Stalin still reads a good deal, including numerous books translated for him and the Politburo, which the public never sees. He
also reads daily translations of the foreign press. There is evi-

dence that he often reads correspondents' dispatches before they are put on the wire. He likes American movies and sees many first-run Hollywood pictures in the Kremlin cinema. It was said that after he saw the U. S. Army production, *The Battle for Russia*, he was so impressed that he ordered the Stalin prize withheld from a similar Soviet production, to which it was to have been awarded.

He studies assiduously in many branches of knowledge and he has the help of experts always in readiness for consultation. I never met anyone who talked to him who was not surprised by his ready fund of information on a wide variety of subjects, his ability to ask searching and highly pertinent questions, and his great capacity to listen. When a stranger comes to see him he sits down wearing a poker face, and says nothing, waiting for the other to go to the heart of business at once. After the guest has finished talking Stalin lifts his head and gives an answer or begins to talk himself.

When warmed up to a subject he is a forceful and shrewd conversationalist. He has a good sense of earthy humor, at times rather puckish, or with a biting edge of satire or sarcasm to it. It is well known how he mercilessly goaded Churchill, during the latter's first visit to Moscow. "What are you afraid of?" he asked the Prime Minister. "Those Germans aren't nearly as tough as you think. See how well we have been getting along all by ourselves? Your information about them is all wrong. Just jump across the Channel and try them out." And so on.

At one point Churchill became so incensed that he ordered his plane to prepare to leave immediately, though the business of the conference had hardly begun. Stalin's weather bureau simply told him the heavens wouldn't permit it; besides, he must stay for a banquet. Churchill got even by wearing his siren suit to the banquet. He remained slumped in his seat when Sir Archibald Clark-Kerr proposed a toast to Stalin, and he publicly reprimanded His Majesty's Ambassador for not first toasting Molotov—the minister to whom he was accredited. But

Churchill swallowed his pride and in later meetings the two men, so opposite in nearly every characteristic, came to respect each other. Perhaps there is now a certain reluctant affection between them, but Winston still waxes irascible under an occasional Stalinist sarcasm.

Stalin likes a good story but only to illustrate a point. He is himself no raconteur. At meetings with Churchill and the late President it was always Stalin, people present have said, who brought the talk back from wit and anecdotes to the practical affairs under consideration; he hates to leave questions dangling without a decision. He has rather a heavy sense of dignity, and never "plays," apparently. Somebody started an anecdote to the effect that Pat Hurley coached Stalin before he entered the conference room at Teheran and greeted Winston and Franklin. He was supposed to have parted the curtains and said, in English, "What in hell goes on here?" It is an amusing addition to the Hurley legend, but needless to say it is apocryphal.

Stalin's public speeches during the war have been few, but they are certainly the most readable and most important documents published in the country. He had, of course, the great advantage of being able to say precisely what he meant, without fear of contradiction. He wastes few words on rhetoric, but when he wants to press home a point he usually draws on a homely epigram, or an aphorism understood by every Russian. He is direct to the extent of bluntness or rudeness. He likes candor in other people too—as our former naval attaché in Moscow, Rear Admiral John Duncan, discovered one night at a Kremlin feast.

Toasts had been made to practically everything but the kitchen sink when Stalin stood up and offered his respects to the intelligence services of the armed forces. He said that no army could win battles without a good intelligence service. As an example he pointed to the British campaign in Gallipoli, in World War One. The British had won it, if they had only known; the Turks had already decided to retreat from the height which dominated the battle, when unexpectedly the British withdrew. The implication was plain—Stalin was harping on British exaggeration of the dangers of a landing in France.

The British naval attaché, an admiral seated at the main table with Stalin, turned crimson but said nothing. Jack Duncan, segregated at a side table because he was then still a captain, fumed within himself till he could contain his wrath no longer. Whereupon he arose, knocked on his glass, and proposed a counter-toast.

"What the Premier has just said about the importance of intelligence services is all very true," opined Duncan. "But in order to be effective, an intelligence officer has to have the co-operation of his allies. Here in Russia it is my duty to collect information useful to the winning of the war against our common enemy, yet I have found nobody willing to help me do that job." And more of same. Astonished at his own audacity, Duncan sat down in a hushed room.

After hearing a translation Stalin smiled broadly, got up, walked the full length of his own table and crossed the room to Duncan's seat. There he laughed, clinked glasses with him, and then turned and said to his guests:

"Now here is a man I understand. He says exactly what he is thinking. I like a man like that. Captain Duncan, from now on I will be your intelligence officer."

After dinner Stalin drew Duncan aside, still smiling, and brought him together with the chief of the Red Fleet. "Give this man the facts he needs," said Stalin. The young captain didn't actually get much new information afterwards, but anyway our Navy made him an admiral a month later.

Although momentous new events have occurred since 1941, and new and undreamed-of changes in power relationships, no official attempt was made to examine and interpret their significance, in terms of theoretical Marxism. No comprehensive Marxist analysis appeared in Russia to explain, for example, how this conflict, which was first described as "the Second Imperialist

War," and after the Nazi invasion became the Patriotic War, developed into a coalition between the largest and most powerful "bourgeois capitalist-imperialist nations" and the world's only socialist state. The Communist conception of the next general war had always been based on Lenin's prediction of an "inevitable" encirclement and attack on the Soviet Union by the combined world bourgeoisie. No complete formulation or modification of the classic Marxist-Leninist theses on the imperialist war, taking in all new contemporary phenomena, has yet been attempted.

Issued in the tens of millions, Stalin's war-time speeches remain virtually the only basic text reconciling past dectrine to the Soviet state's present alliance with the "imperialist" nations. All these speeches are, of course, intensely practical. "Theoretical vagaries have never led, and never can lead, to any good," says Stalin. And in this period perhaps the keynote of his own thinking, in synthesizing his Marxist training with the present situation, was struck when he emphasized in discussing the "fighting alliance" with Britain and America, that "the logic of *things* is stronger than any other logic"; it is stronger than any ideological theory as such.

During the war Stalin enormously increased his own burden, and assumed direct responsibility for all the most important phases of national life and national defense. For many years the only nominal basis of his political power rested in his position as Secretary-General of the Communist Party. But 1945 found him Chairman of the Council of Peoples Commissars (the equivalent of Premier), Supreme Commander-in-Chief, Commissar of National Defense, Deputy to the Supreme Soviet and member of its Presidium. He is also Chairman of the State Defense Committee of the USSR.

In all those jobs Stalin is the active directing chief, and beyond them he intervenes in a personal way in countless other aspects of Soviet life. Even such a little thing as the restoration of the "soft sign" in Russian orthography, for example, is credited to

him. Numerous old traditions and institutions associated with
pre-revolutionary national patriotism have been revived at his
initiative. He has not hesitated to ignore doctrinaire prejudices
and party axioms whenever events showed them to be interfering with practical results in war or production.

It is known that the broad lines of Red Army strategy were
approved and in part devised by Stalin, and that many measures
of improvement and reorganization stemmed from him. At the
outbreak of the war Marshal Voroshilov and Marshal Shaposni-
kov were chiefly relied upon to determine strategy and organizational matters. After early disasters Stalin brought in the younger
and more pliant and resourceful Marshals Zhukov and Vasilev-
sky, who revivified the Red Army. In close consultation with
them, it is said, Stalin worked out the details of the defense of
Stalingrad and the general plan for the victorious counter-
offensive.

The defense of Moscow and Leningrad, too, probably owed
much to Stalin's personal decisions. How much responsibility he
bore for the lavish and somewhat Asiatic use of manpower for
the achievement of limited objectives, which characterized much
of Russian conduct of the war, it is impossible to know. But
Stalin at least must have sanctioned the sacrifice of thousands of
half-trained civilian militiamen in the costly salvation of Moscow. They went to certain death, but the few hours they held
the German panzers back enabled the Siberian troops to reach
the city and win that critical battle. In the case of Leningrad,
the Red Army staff had originally intended to withdraw and
fight on another line. Reading through Russian history Stalin
came upon a reference to Peter the Great's plan to hold Leningrad by artillery alone. He was said to have been so much impressed that he called upon his staff to answer Peter's arguments.
Zhukov agreed with Peter and it was decided to hold Leningrad
against siege.

But the degree to which Stalin's personal sagacity affected
Russia's military success is, after all, not the most important

thing. What mattered was that he had the wisdom to pick capable marshals and to give them very great authority, and that
he knew how to pool their advice and co-ordinate it in the
mobilization of all the broad political and economic and moral
means at his disposal, in order to win victory.

Stalin's own coolness did somewhat inspire confidence at the
nadir of Russian morale, after the loss of the Ukraine and during
the battle for Moscow. When the Germans were on the edge of
the capital Stalin stayed on in the Kremlin. Again, many doubted
that a second front would ever be opened by Russia's allies.
Stalin assured them that it would be—at the same time he mocked
Churchill for the long "delay." For theoretical reasons many
Russians believed that a coalition with the capitalist powers
could not be stabilized. They thought the latter would seek a
separate peace, once the Red Army had been bled enough. Before the Teheran Conference some party men urged Stalin to
beat the "imperialists" to it, and accept Hitler's peace offers. But
the Soviet leader reproved these Satanic voices and reassured
the nation that the coalition was dependable and would survive
the war.

In America, Stalin is often thought of as the most powerful
"isolationist" or "nationalist" force in Russia, and too narrowly
Marxist in his views to believe in true co-operation with bourgeois states. That he is a profound skeptic need not be questioned, but that his practical sense overrides his skepticism is
obvious. Events compelled him to make commitments to Roosevelt and Churchill, leaders of the oft-denounced "imperialist nations," despite the deep distrust, and very probably against the
advice, of many of his proletarian colleagues. Americans seldom
appreciate Stalin's role as the focus of conflicting "isolationist"
and "internationalist" sentiment inside the Soviet Union, comparable to our own division of opinion. It has been no easy task
for him to reconcile the really extreme isolationists in his own
camp to the support of international agreements made on a new
plane, full of possibilities contradicting pre-war Marxist theory

—possibilities upon which dogmatists never dreamed of speculating.

In a statement of the essence of this battle for the world which sharply illuminated the difference between the ideologies involved, the chief Soviet marshal declared, in November, 1944:

"The strength of Soviet patriotism lies in the fact that it is based not on racial or nationalistic prejudices, but on the people's profound devotion and loyalty to their homeland, on the fraternal partnership of the working people of all the nationalities in our land. . . . It is not only a military defeat that the Hitlerites have sustained in this war, but moral and political defeat as well. The ideology of equality of all races and nations which has taken firm root in our country, the ideology of friendship among the peoples, has emerged completely victorious over the Hitlerite ideology of bestial nationalism and racial hatred."

This assertion must have brought deep satisfaction to Stalin, for here he proclaimed a personal triumph as well. As a Georgian (he still speaks Russian with a marked accent) and as a member of one of the minor nationalities himself, he keenly resented the old Tsarist habit of racial discrimination and the promotion of pogroms. As early as 1912 he wrote a book setting forth his own ideas on the subject, which was highly praised by Lenin. Later on it became a fundamental policy, written into the Soviet constitution.

Whatever one may say about the lack of personal freedom and individual liberty under his regime—and very much indeed can be said against it—there is no doubt that realization of the principle of racial and national equality inside the Soviet Union is in line with the best traditions of democracy. Stalin was quite right in attributing much of Soviet Russia's strength to that policy. Given application in terms of fullest recognition of the equality of sovereign rights and independence of all nations, this principle might well become the foundation on which President Truman could meet Stalin and Churchill to unite the world in an effective peace.

IV
Mechanics of Rule

STALIN has become so much a synonym for the Soviet Union, both inside Russia and beyond, that many people think his whims and fantasies are literally the only rule the nation knows. Russia is a dictatorship; Stalin is a dictator; ergo, Russia is Stalin. So the logic goes. American publicists and commentators, with their habit of asking questions like "What does Stalin think?" and "What will Stalin do?"—and they always seem to know— give us the impression that everything is decided by Joseph Vissarionovich Ivanovich David Nijeradse Chizhkov Dzhugashvili, to use his real and full name, with all known patronymics. Very happily this was changed, at Lenin's suggestion long before the Revolution, to the present simple "Stalin," which means steel.

Uncle Joe, as he is known to millions overseas, but not among Russians, decides a tremendous lot, of course, and no change in policy occurs without his sanction. There is now only one He in Russia and Stalin is it. But there are limits to his ubiquity and power, even though you might not suspect it from reading the Soviet press. Thousands of decisions are made that never cross his desk, and many of them are important.

While it is often difficult to see the legal basis for much of Stalin's power, and that of the Communist Party itself, it is interesting to note that Stalin considers he is the agent of the people, in a broad sense. In distinction to the totalitarian conception, he admits, in theory at least, that all power stems from the consent of the governed.

163

"A deputy should know," he told the citizens of Moscow when he was up for election in 1937, "that he is a servant of the people, their emissary in the Supreme Soviet, and that he must follow the line laid down in the mandate given him by the people. If he turns off the road, the electors are entitled to demand new elections, and as to the deputy who turned off the road, they have the right to send him packing."

But he evidently saw no contradiction between that statement and his own definition of the role of the Communist Party:

> No important political or organizational problem is ever decided by our soviets and other mass organizations without directives from our party. In this sense we may say that the dictatorship of the proletariat is, substantially, the dictatorship of the party, as the force which effectively guides.

The explanation is that to Stalin the party is synonymous with "the mandate of the people" and that he is its instrument. Thus, he regards all his decisions as products of collective party judgment.

About twenty million people, including Communists and Young Communists, are pledged to enforce that "proletarian dictatorship," and the majority of them never see Stalin himself. The machinery consists of hundreds of little party committees, each of which has its own little leader, and each of which, on its own level, rules the daily lives of the average peasant and worker.

At the highest level, in Moscow, the apparatus is also run by committees. And it is in his position as undisputed leader standing at the apex of a vast party complex, reaching into all the recesses of the Soviet Union, that Stalin has power of final judgment. Because he is also a national symbol, an institution, a state property in a sense, in whom the party has deliberately built up the personification of its own prestige, there are situations in which he does not have as much freedom as the President of the United States.

Roosevelt, for example, did not ask his Cabinet's permission

when he chose to go abroad. In declining to attend the Quebec
Conference, Stalin explained that his Government—really the
Politburo—thought it undesirable that he should leave at that
moment. Very likely Stalin also sought and accepted Politburo
advice about the timing of his assumption of the title Supreme
Commander-in-Chief of the Red Army. It was no accident that
this came about just before the reversal of the whole tide of
battle, at Stalingrad, and not during the critical time of the
Battle of Moscow.

"The decisions of single persons," said Stalin, in rejecting the
Führer principle of personal dictatorship, "are always, or nearly
always, one-sided. Out of every one hundred decisions made by
single persons, that have not been tested and corrected collec-
tively, ninety are one-sided. In our leading body, the Central
Committee of our party, which guides all our soviet and party
organizations, there are about seventy members. Each one is
able to contribute his experience. Were it otherwise, if decisions
had been taken by individuals, we should have committed very
serious mistakes."

It was interesting to note that when Stalin delivered what was
perhaps his most impressive war-time speech in November, 1942,
he prefaced it with the statement that he had been "instructed"
—presumably by TSEKA—to make that report to the nation. The
Central Committee, or TSEKA, which Stalin says holds the
"combined wisdom of the party," is elected by all-union Communist congresses held periodically. Now there is an annual all-
union party conference which can also add or dismiss TSEKA
members. Inside TSEKA itself is the small Political Bureau
(Politburo) in which is concentrated the decisive policy-making
and administrative power of the nation. The eight members (besides Stalin) of the Politburo, and the five alternate members,
are always at the chief marshal's right and left hands. Each carries enormous responsibilities, and together they shape destiny
across more than one-fifth of the earth. It is significant that in its
membership the Politburo includes representatives of most of

the major nationalities of the Soviet Union. There is, however, no member from Central Asia or Siberia—though Kazakhs, Uzbeks and other Asiatics are included in the Central Committee, just beneath the parent family.

It is a long, tortuous climb to the Politburo. Unlike politics in this country, the possibility of a swift dark horse rising to the top is virtually nil. The Politburo is stabilized now, and no new member is likely to arrive there, within Stalin's time, and acquire sufficient power to become a figure of utmost importance. From among its present faces, therefore, will some day come Joseph Stalin's successor—an ever-present possibility which must have been borne home to all of them with closer emphasis when Franklin D. Roosevelt suddenly slipped away.

Let us learn something about these men around Stalin, then—or as much as we can learn from a foreigner's seat in the Soviet Union, which is at best somewhere in the first balcony.

CHAPTER TEN

Men of the Kremlin

I

The World's Most Exclusive Society

COMPARED to other members of the Politburo, Stalin's life is an open book. Except for Foreign Minister Vyacheslav Mikhailovich Molotov, who occasionally grants a press interview when the Government has a statement of unusual importance to issue, they rarely see foreign newspaper men, and never for quotation. So little is known about these men in the outer world, however, that even morsels of information casually acquired during a year in Russia may help us to understand how that country is run.

The fact is, the home of no Vanderbilt or Astor, and certainly not Buckingham Palace, was ever so difficult to enter as it is to cross the threshold of a Politburo member. No British or American diplomat has ever been invited to the private home of any one of them—again, Molotov excepted. It is his job to entertain foreigners. Also, few officials' wives appear at public receptions. Women are not as a rule invited to the state banquets Stalin gives for visiting brass hats. Outside Lhassa, this is the most exclusively male government in the world.

Of all the elite society in which the somewhat blasé Kathy Harriman doubtless has circulated, she was never in such exclusive company as the night her ambassador father brought her to the ballet arranged for Churchill. When Stalin entered the box, she was the only lady present, in a host of high officials. Miss

167

Harriman herself was fully aware of the situation, as the theater stared.

"That's the first time," a colleague sitting beside me remarked, "that anyone ever saw Kathy *beam.*"

But while no foreign diplomat has ever been able to call Stalin or any other Politburo member by his first name, there is one place where everything about these men is known and recorded. They live in a goldfish bowl as far the NKVD is concerned. They are at all times under the protection of NKVD guards. This applies even to Stalin. When Clark-Kerr complained to the Foreign Office about the inevitable plain-clothesmen who follow him wherever he goes, Molotov laughed and said he had to put up with the same thing himself.

Once I made out a questionnaire, hoping to get answers from the NKVD, about members of the Politburo. I wanted to know simple and innocent things such as these: Each man's real and full name? Where educated? Knowledge of foreign languages? Did he ever go hungry? When and whom did he marry? How many children? Does he smoke? What are his working hours? What is his hobby? And so on.

You won't find the answers in the stiff, official biographies, of course, nor in the Soviet press. You might think it harmless enough, but my questions astonished the Russians, and it was no dice.

"Things like that can't possibly be of any interest to foreigners," replied dark, bureaucratic A. A. Petrov, the Chinese-language student who headed the Narkomindel's Press Department.

I had to get the information in other ways, and it was hard digging. Russians are only slightly less reluctant to talk about Politburo chiefs than they are to discuss Stalin as an ordinary human being. Somehow, to them it seems to smack faintly of espionage or disloyalty. So I had to put together this mosaic bit by bit; and while I believe all the features of it are accurate, if there are mistakes, Mr. Petrov has no one to blame but himself.

II

The Super-Cabinet

ALL THESE men of the Kremlin have a common background. They are almost without exception the sons of peasants or workers whose parents could not read or write. Out of their bitter impoverished youth came early revolutionary activity. Many of them spent years in political imprisonment or exile. Mastery of the science of revolution, and of the manipulation of revolutionary power, has been their goal all their lives. To that they have subordinated everything—absolutely everything. Nearly all of them, at one time or another, held important positions in the Communist International, and helped plan world revolution.

Their working day runs from ten to fourteen hours; as a rule they rise late and, like Stalin, do their business in the afternoon and far into the night. One exception is Kalinin. Another is Lazar Moisseyevich Kaganovich, who unsnarled the Soviet railways. He also built the Moscow subway and his name is engraved over every entrance to it. He is said to rise at five-thirty and study between six and nine. Almost entirely self-taught, he is one of the ablest technical administrators in Russia. Incidentally he is the only Jew in the Politburo; and his wife, a very capable woman and also Jewish, is chairman of the Soviet textile workers trade union.

All seem to lead morally conservative lives. Like all Russians, most of them enjoy good food, vodka and wine. None has any personal wealth or investments, but they have the best living quarters in the country, abundant food allowances, motor cars and luxurious offices. Most of them live in the Kremlin. Most of them are family men, but little is heard of their wives. Their children attend ordinary public schools, though they are taken to and from them by uniformed chauffeurs.

Andrei Alexandrovich Zhdanov and Alexander Sergeyevich Shcherbakov (who is Zhdanov's brother-in-law) are both corpulent men—which is considered a political handicap in the Soviet Union. Most of the others are spare or middling in size, and have exceptional physical stamina. Nearly all are short; Kaganovich and Shcherbakov are the only ones who tower above Stalin. Mikhail Ivanovich Kalinin, Chairman of the Presidium of the Supreme Soviet, is the oldest; he is seventy. Stalin is sixty-six; and Marshal Klementi Efremovich Voroshilov is next, at sixty-four. The youngest member is Nicholai Ivanovich Voznessensky, who is in his early forties.

Nobody could be more naive than some foreign diplomats who fancy they are getting an "influence" in the Kremlin because Stalin and Molotov have been cordial to them a few times. Personal relations even with Russians move these men very little, when recognition of them demands any departure from the "logic of things." Several have seen close family relatives go into political exile. They pride themselves on being men of iron and they live only for their work and survive only by getting practical results. They are dedicated to the state, and to the power that they control—which in turn controls them.

I keep remembering an incident which perhaps conveys the code by which these men live better than anything else. It was at a diplomatic function and I was speaking to a commissar who is a puissant figure just below the top level. A remark was made which could, by vastly exaggerating the merest hint of an implication, have been interpreted to suggest that he was personally interested in a certain young lady. Instantly he frowned severely, and made what seemed to me, until later reflection, a wholly irrelevant rejoinder.

"I have no time for play and no time for fun," he said very

slowly. "I have no time for vodka, for women, or for song. I live for my work—work—work."

"Relax, you're among friends," I felt like saying to him. But he was in dead earnest. As a man with a terrific power drive, who has not yet fully arrived, he is probably more of a robot than the big men directly above him, who seem human enough, when you meet them. But they all got where they are by that same formula, which is the complete antithesis of lazy, easy-going Tsarist officials of the past.

The Politburo is not, of course, the Government *per se*. It is not a cabinet, in our sense; the equivalent of that is the Council of People's Commissars, which is made up of the chairmen of the forty-one all-union commissariats, and of the committees on arts, higher schools and state planning. The Politburo is, instead, a super-cabinet, and each member is responsible for issuing party directives to one or more commissariats. He may or not may be its formal head. The only other government I know with a similar organic construction is the Koumintang regime in China—which borrowed the edifice wholesale from Russia, when Dr. Sun Yat-sen made his alliance with Moscow.

Few changes have occurred in Politburo membership for the past decade, except for the election of new alternate members and the replacement of several men purged in 1937. There are now five so-called "New Bolsheviks" (party members after the Revolution began), as follows: Lavrenti Pavlovich Beria, a Georgian, head of the NKVD and Home Affairs, who is answerable for internal security and a huge amount of industry run by the state police and its involuntary workers, including war prisoners; Nikita Sergeyevich Krushchev, a Ukrainian, leader of the Ukrainian Party and Premier of the Ukrainian Republic; Anastas Ivanovich Mikoyan, an Armenian, who organized the Soviet food industry, and is also head of the Foreign Trade Commissariat; A. S. Shcherbakov, secretary of the Moscow party committee, head of the political department of the Red Army, chief of Soviet propaganda, and thus comptroller of the press; and N. Y. Voznessensky, an economic expert who heads Gosplan and co-ordinates all state planning.

No member of the Politburo had an extensive formal education. Stalin and Molotov both know a little German; so does Kaganovich. None of them speaks English, though Stalin knows a few words and others are now, like many Russian officials, studying the language of their chief allies. Stalin, Voroshilov, Kalinin, Molotov, Kaganovich, Mikoyan and Zhdanov have all been outside the Soviet Union, but only briefly. Only Molotov and Mikoyan have seen either Britain or America.

Mikoyan, at least, frankly set America as the model for Soviet light industries and public services to emulate. At the last party congress in 1939 he was the only speaker, in fact, who waxed enthusiastic about the achievements of American industry. In the same speech, incidentally, he praised Stalin's name over forty times in the first 2,000 words. He is a great favorite with the marshal—and also with workers in his commissariat. Every Russian knows him as the man who introduced modern canning and frozen foods to the Soviet Union. He dresses well, has a scintillating personality, likes to dance, and is said to have been quite a ladies' man, a reputation now ably upheld by his two dashing sons. Mikoyan, vice-chairman of the Council of People's Commissars and member of the State Defense Committee, is a man of first-line importance.

Many of these busy men do not see their families for days. Zhdanov, however, has always made it a point to spend at least one hour every day with his son, who is said to be a brilliant young man. The elder Zhdanov is considered the "intellectual" of the Kremlin. He is the only Politburo member who had the equivalent of a college education, and his wife is also a well-educated Russian. Zhdanov knows French and German. He once wrote a highly critical essay about Shostakovich's style of composition, which resulted in the latter's temporary eclipse in Soviet music. More of him, in a moment.

III

The Old Guard

HENRY CASSIDY, an exceptionally well-informed correspondent on Russia and one to whom Stalin has shown several favors, is inclined to think that the Premier is beginning to feel his years, and that this has already become a growingly conservative influence on him. Cassidy reasons that Stalin is too old now to wish to undertake any risky experiments or embark on hazardous ventures abroad. He wants his last years to be remembered as an era of peace, of consolidation of all the gains made in his time; he wants to see a harvest of the toil and tears spent in planting the seeds of socialism. "If I live that long—" is now frequently a preface to Stalin's remarks about the future.

Cassidy's surmise may be correct, but so far Stalin has shown no sign of relinquishing any corner of his unique position. Like Lenin, he has never publicly spoken of a successor, or indicated one, and Russians are naturally shy about speculating on the subject. On the basis of seniority in party history, however, the first five names would be: Kalinin, Voroshilov, Molotov, Shvernik and Kaganovich.

Kalinin and Voroshilov are probably ruled out by age alone; Stalin stands a good chance of outlasting them. In recent years Voroshilov has taken a back seat, but both he and Kalinin remain popular figures. As chairman, or president, of the Presidium of the Supreme Soviet, Kalinin is still nominally head of the state, the kindly grandfather figure known to millions of peasants. He writes innumerable letters—some eighty thousand in one year—and personally shakes hands with thousands of humble people who come to see him from all over the Union. He also greets all diplomats in the name of the state. Except for Sverdlov, a Jew who was President of the Central Executive Committee of the Communist Party in 1919, Kalinin has been head of the Presidium of the Supreme Soviet ever since the revolution. He is still in fair health, which he takes care to preserve.

Nikolai Mikhailovich Shvernik, another Old Bolshevik, has for many years been vice-chairman of the Presidium of the Supreme Soviet. He is generally expected to succeed to the presidency, when Kalinin dies or retires. A man who favors regular working hours and living habits, Shvernik does not smoke and rarely takes a drink. At the celebration of the twenty-fifth anniversary of the October Revolution, he was observed to toast only in lemonade.

Molotov is now perhaps the best-known Russian name, after the big chief's, outside the Soviet Union, and even inside the country he is often considered No. 2 man. In his entire career he has never wavered in his loyalty to Stalin. Stalin has delegated great responsibility to him and there is probably nobody in the Government whom he trusts more. Before Stalin took over, Molotov was Premier, as well as president of STO, the Council of Labor and Defense, which has a key function of control inside the state apparatus. Now he is first vice-chairman (there are six) of the Council of Commissars, besides being head of the Narkomindel, or Commissariat of Foreign Affairs, where he replaced Maxim Litvinov.

Molotov means "sledge-hammer"; his real name is Skriabin and he is a nephew of the famous composer. A short, compact figure, his manner and appearance suggest a stern meticulous schoolmaster—an impression strengthened by his pince-nez—but beneath his pedantic exterior he is all Bolshevik. Men under him work long, exacting hours. He is an exceptionably able and conscientious administrator. He rode through the great Purge tri-

umphantly and probably nobody in the Government today feels
more secure. He would seem indispensable for any Politburo.

Molotov's wife was for a time also a figure of power in party
politics, as a candidate member of the Central Committee. She
started the Soviet perfume industry and was head of the cos-
metics trust. They have two daughters. The eldest, Svetlana,
led the list of honor pupils at her public school when I visited
there. Another honor pupil at the same school, incidentally, was
the lovely adopted Chinese daughter of Georgi Dmitrov, once
secretary-general of the Comintern, who still lives in the Kremlin.

Molotov had an opportunity to see Britain and America in
1941, long before he dreamed of becoming a chairman of the
San Francisco Conference. The most he is known to have revealed of his impressions, however, was during a visit to Buckingham Palace. "Things are quite different here," he laconically
remarked to the British monarch, "from what I had imagined."
While in England, too, Molotov explained to Churchill that the
revival of some symbols of Russian nationalism had been more
successful than anticipated, and that more steps of a similar
nature were contemplated.

"There's still a lot of the old Adam left in the Russian, eh?"
said Churchill, his eyes twinkling beneath shaggy brows. Molotov quickly explained that Russian patriotism in this war was
quite different from anything in the past. It was the new Soviet
patriotism.

But the Soviet bureaucracy is not the self-contained colossus
that the old Tsarist one was, and prominent office in itself is no
sure measure of internal power. The main thing is the individual's position in the party organization and the degree of confidence reposed in him. There is a very good indication of this,
in the membership of the key party organs. Besides the Politburo,
the Central Committee has two other juntas of high power. One
is the party secretariat, of four members; the other is the party
organization bureau (Orgburo), of nine. Molotov, Kalinin,

Voroshilov and Kaganovich are not members of either one. Seats in both are held only by Stalin, Zhdanov, Andreyev and Malenkov. Andreyev is, besides, chairman of the Party Control Commission, which can "fire" any Communist.

IV

Heirs Apparent

DURING Stalins absence in Teheran, the old head of the anti-God movement, Yaroslavsky, was called to what must, presumably, have been a very lively reward. Members of the Politburo were his pallbearers. Russians attached importance to whose name was listed first. One list was headed by Andreyev—but another, it was said, by Malenkov. Ordinarily, Politburo members are mentioned alphabetically.

Andreyev will be fifty this year, Zhdanov will be forty-nine, Malenkov is only forty-four, and all are in excellent health. None of them is an Old Bolshevik. Zhdanov and Andreyev joined the party in their teens, during World War One; Malenkov became a party member only in 1920. All three have always been loyal to Stalin, since he came to the top. In Andreyev's case there was a brief "deviation" many years ago, presumably now completely forgotten. He once opposed Lenin and Stalin over a question of party control; he wanted labor unions to run Soviet industry.

Many Russians consider that Andreyev and Zhdanov, in whom Stalin reposes deep trust combined with high party responsibility, are probably the most powerful figures in the Union, after him. Stalin relies on their judgment and depends upon them to keep the party apparatus functioning smoothly. Neither man is much known to foreigners and very little appears about them in the press. But both are respected and feared in the party. They are opposites in personality, appearance and—for once—in early background.

Andrei Andreyevich Andreyev is an unusual name. In English it would be Andrew Andrewson Andrews, II. He is a small man, the shortest of them all, but of great vitality and endurance. In his youth he was a shepherd, then a hired farm laborer, later a railway worker. He had only two years of schooling, but in the rough-and-tumble fight for domination of labor, during the Revolution, he became party boss of the railway union. He sided with Stalin at the right time, and helped turn all labor against Zinoviev, Trotsky and Kamenev.

Andreyev's face reminds many people of Earl Browder. But he is seldom seen in public places and almost never in the theater. He still dresses in the old party uniform which Stalin also wore before he became a marshal. It is a severely cut garment, with a high stiff collar, of black material in winter, and white linen in summer. In most cases this has now given way to more colorful apparel, led off by Stalin's gold-braided marshal's uniform, with its diamond neck-star.

Tovarishch Andreyev probably can call more comrades by their first names than anybody except Malenkov, who, as head of the Orgburo, is an equally potent figure. "Malenkov's brain is a huge card index of party members," one Russian Communist told me, "and on demand he can supply the personal history of anyone Stalin asks about." He knows the state bureaucracy inside out, and is the active boss of it.

Malenkov is probably the most powerful of the vice-chairmen of the Council of Commissars. He issues directives to heavy industry and picks key men to head it. During the war he concentrated especially on the construction of tanks; mostly for success in this effort he was awarded the high decoration, Hero of Socialist Labor.

As chairman of the Party Control Commission, all Commun-

ists must reckon with Andreyev. Besides that powerful super-
visory role, his chief responsibility is agriculture, in which he is
a self-educated expert. Stalin used him to whip the party machine through the collectivization period—to its harsh, and ultimately completely victorious, conclusion. After the German
attack it was Andreyev's duty to see that agriculture met the
demands of the war. Heads of all the state and collective farm
groups are answerable to him.

Zhdanov would make two of Andreyev, and he is said to be so
disturbed by his bulk that he fasts and diets, something very
rare for a Russian. In his official biography there is no mention
of his ever having been a worker or peasant; evidently he went
direct from school into full-time party work, another rare thing
for a top Soviet figure. His father also was an able and intelligent
man and it is possible he came from the petty bourgeoisie. If so,
he identified himself completely with the cause of the proletariat, and his record as a Stalinist is absolutely *sans* blemish.

Zhdanov has risen step by step, through the party apparatus,
much as Stalin rose: doing small jobs in the Urals first, then in
Nizhegoredsky, then in Gorky. He did not become a member of
the Central Committee till 1930, and only in 1934 was elected
alternate member in the Politburo. It was then, after the assassination of Kirov, Stalin's closest friend, that Zhdanov emerged
in the front line. He became secretary of the Leningrad party
committee, to succeed Kirov, in a job which Stalin has regarded
as most important, ever since Zinoviev used his position there to
try to overthrow him.

Besides holding down Leningrad during the war, and organizing its defense during the blockade, Zhdanov has taken many
party problems off Stalin's hands. He wears the stars of a colonel-
general in the Red Army and thus in military rank is second only
to Stalin and Voroshilov in the Politburo. In this job he maintains party control of the Army. With the assistance of his
brother-in-law, Shcherbakov, he was responsible for co-ordinating party and military affairs. Here it may be emphasized that

none of the new Red Army marshals, no military figure of the war, has been able to break into the ranks of the party supreme command, not even Zhukov. Just the contrary is true, as indicated by Stalin's own assumption of marshal's rank, together with the creation of four other Politburo generals.

Zhdanov is an able speaker and a forceful writer, who seldom wastes words. He speaks with intrepidity and confidence. His remarks are clear and purposeful, and little touched by the repetitive quotations and eulogies of Stalin with which most Soviet officials interlard whatever comment they make. At the last party congress Zhdanov seemed surer than anyone else of what he wanted to say, perhaps because it had all been approved in advance by Stalin. At any rate, he struck out boldly with original ideas and criticism. Very often he said "I think" where others would only venture an opinion as "Stalin says." His smooth-flowing prose style on the whole makes brisk, informative and interesting reading, enlivened by humor and wit, and is surprisingly close to Stalin's own.

It was Zhdanov who was chosen to draft the revised rules for the Bolshevik Party—most important since the changes a generation ago during the NEP period. He is credited with having done much, under Stalin's direction, to bind up the wounds left in the party body after the great purge of 1937. Before the last congress he frankly declared:

"The objectionable feature of the mass purges was that, bearing as they do the character of a campaign, they are attended by many mistakes, primarily by infringement of the Leninist principle of an individual approach to people. . . . There were numerous cases of hostile elements who had wormed their way into the party, taking advantage of the purges to persecute and ruin honest people. There is no necessity for the method of the mass purge."

Amendments to the party rules, which Zhdanov proposed, helped to restore surviving members' sense of security, and brought about some return to democracy within the party. Mem-

bers can no longer be expelled in secret sessions, without a
chance to defend themselves in open party meetings; and it is
now written into party law that any member has a right to appeal
his case to the Central Committee itself.

As spokesman for the TSEKA, Zhdanov championed the
broader recognition of youth in the party, made it easier for
young people to enter, and did away with some of the tyrannous
practices of older bureaucrats. He led a demand for admission
of Young Communists to full party membership at the age of
eighteen, which is now the case. In general his recommendations
encouraged party expansion, resulting in the present unprecedented membership of about five million—the great majority of
them products of post-revolutionary Russia.

Zhdanov himself may be said to have matured entirely under
the influence of the new state, and thus represents, on the highest political plateau overlooking the nation, a generation very
different from Stalin's own. "As Stalin symbolizes the period of
revolutionary struggle and change," one Communist explained
to me, "Zhdanov symbolizes socialism as the period lying in between revolution and the coming period of Communism."

In 1944, the colonel-general's political responsibilities reached
beyond the borders of the Soviet Union when Stalin delegated
him to sign the military treaty with Finland, and sent him to
Helsinki to head the Allied Control Commission there. Under
Zhdanov Finnish labor came to the fore, and pro-Soviet organizations were created to help shape Finland's policy toward
permanent alliance.

But of course all sorts of things could happen to interrupt such
a promising career. In any case Stalin, though slowing up somewhat, seems good for many years yet. He has now outlived
Roosevelt and seems almost certain to outlive Churchill. And as
long as he is vigorously alive, no one in Russia would publicly
speak of a successor—last of all Zhdanov.

Among the things which drew Zhdanov to Stalin was the
younger man's close friendship with Kirov. The three of them

collaborated in the first moves toward revising the teaching of Russian history, so as to glorify the past. Together they wrote a book called *On the Recreation of History,* which was the beginning of the wholesale revival of Russian traditions and institutions. This movement has, by now, reached immense proportions, which may end in changing all but the economic foundations of Soviet—as well as world—socialism. We have already noticed some of these changes in earlier chapters. Now I am going to attempt to summarize what they mean in the daily life of the Soviet citizen.

CHAPTER ELEVEN

Russia Rediscovers Her Past

I

The Drama of Change

EVERYONE knows that dramatic social changes have taken place in Russia during the war. Many innovations of the "proletarian state" have been discarded in favor of institutions, customs and methods traditionally associated with Great Russian nationalism, and formerly rejected as reflections of "petty-bourgeois or bourgeois prejudices." Along with such restorations flows an ever-widening stream of historical connection between revolutionary and pre-revolutionary times, so that in a sense the younger generation is rediscovering the Russian past.

There is a larger religious freedom in Russia now, and the Church has recovered important privileges. Marriage laws have become far more strict, as we have seen; divorce is very difficult to obtain. A sterner moral tone in general prevails, and there is increased emphasis on dignity and more formal manners, and on what used to be scorned as bourgeois etiquette. The individual family again is idealized, and parental responsibility stressed in the training of youth. Instead of huge apartment houses, to encourage collective living in the cities, many post-war housing and reconstruction projects call for single or duplex or triplex dwellings. Incidentally, architects are now less concerned with experiments in bizzare new forms to express "proletarian culture"; the tendency is to copy or adapt from some of the beautiful old Russian and European buildings.

182

There is a turning back to history for inspiration in every branch of art, and many a tarnished reputation has been rehabilitated. The emphasis is on the "glorious Russian people" and on "Russia's historic past."

In the Russian Army today discipline is as strict as it was in Tsarist times. Differences in clothing, food and wages, between officers and their troops, are more marked than ever. Enlisted men are again frequently called "soldats," a word formerly considered odious, instead of "Red Army man" or "fighter." Epaulettes have come back, numerous decorations have been created in honor of such one-time "feudal" heroes as Kutuzov and Suvorov, and there is lots of gold braid and fancy-work for generals. Informal, semi-formal and formal uniforms are also prescribed for diplomatic officials, another return to bourgeois practice. Several other new uniforms have appeared, with smart outfits for Suvorov cadets, students in *tekhnikums,* and so on.

Drastic revisions in educational practice were introduced in 1943 and 1944. Military training of students is now universal, beginning in the fifth grade. Different requirements in that program for boys and girls were said to be the chief reason for segregating the sexes in the middle schools. The old Tsarist system of grading students has been restored, and gold and silver medals for scholarship, along with graduation and entrance examinations. A set of strict "rules for students" greatly increases discipline. Logic and sociology are back on the curricula, where Marxism alone was once thought to suffice.

What is perhaps more important than any of that, students have sometimes been compelled to abandon their studies and enter the Labor Reserves, or trade schools, or factories, in order to help support dependents at home, while sons and daughters of parents in high-income groups are able to continue their education. This development appears to be attributable to war conditions, however. It will be significant to see whether it is later corrected, or whether the economic position of the parent is to become a permanent factor limiting equality of educational opportunity.

How much do all such changes and tendencies toward social conservatism represent basic departures from the foundational theory and practice of Soviet socialism? One good measure of this can be suggested by a closer examination of the new role assigned to the Church.

II

Controlled "Opium"

MARXISM holds religion to be a reflex action growing out of man's failure to master the material forces of his environment. Friederich Engels predicted that under socialist society, when all kinds of "extraneous forces" had been brought under control by central planning, religion and the Church would "vanish." In 1928, the *Communist International Program* of the Comintern declared:

"One of the most important tasks of the cultural revolution affecting the wide masses is the task of systematically and unswervingly combating religion—the opium of the people. The proletarian government must withdraw all State support from the Church, which is the agency of the former ruling class; it must prevent all church interference in State-organized educational affairs . . . (and it) carries on anti-religious propaganda with all the means at its command. . ."

Such was actually the case in Russia till recently. The Society of the Godless, with branches throughout the Union, militantly crusaded for atheism, supported by the State "with all the means

at its command." All financial help was withdrawn from the
Church, and the 1936 Constitution provided that "the Church
is separated from the state and the school from the Church." The
Constitution recognized "freedom of religious *worship* and freedom of anti-religious propaganda for all citizens," but made no
guarantee of freedom *for* religious propaganda. The Church was
in practice forbidden to publish religious books or periodicals,
and religious instruction could only be given secretly in the
home.

Before the war there was already some relaxation in anti-God
activity, but within the past four years the Church has recovered
some privileges which it seems unlikely again to lose. Immediately after the German invasion the Patriarch of the Orthodox
Church of all the Russias, the late Sergeus, offered his unqualified
support to Marshal Stalin. Millions of rubles were raised by his
followers throughout the country, to buy bonds and war equipment, and to help children and families of Red Army men. In the
Ukraine, some of the clergy were involved in the nationalist
separatist movement which for a time collaborated with the Germans, but the bulk of the Church, under Sergeus, remained
loyal. Many priests in Moscow and other cities were decorated
by the Soviet Government—which was quite unprecedented.

"All friction has disappeared during the war," I was told by
the Metropolitan of Moscow, Nicolai Kurchivsky, who also acts
as secretary to the present Patriarch, Alexei. "The decisive
turning point was the attitude adopted by the Church in the first
days of the war, when it demonstrated its love for the Fatherland
and without asking for anything in return wholeheartedly
backed the Red Army."

Nicolai received me in the Patriarch's quarters of the Church
Synod, located in what was formerly a nobleman's home and
later became the residence of the German Ambassador. He was
a big man with a Slavic brow, Nicolai, dressed in brown silk
robes which emphasized his stoutness; and he was all diplomat.
While we talked an old peasant woman came in and kissed his

hand and said she had walked fifty kilometers to ask for his aid in reopening her village church. And before I left another peasant, an old man with long flying hair and wearing a dirty cloak, a real *muzhik,* went through the same ceremony—and made the same request.

"Are you reopening many churches?" I asked him.

"Quite a few. As fast as we receive permission from the authorities, and they are proving most co-operative."

Nicolai told me there had been 150 churches in Moscow before the Revolution, but only fifty-five were open in 1939. Now there were over sixty, and plans were being made to restore and open several others. In all Russia, he estimated, there were now about 15,000 churches, but as far as I could learn not a single new church had been built since the Revolution. Patriarch Alexei informed me that the Government had promised to help restore, as "historical monuments," many of the shrines destroyed in the occupied areas.

The Synod is now permitted to publish Bibles and other religious books, to manufacture religious vestments for priests and monks, and to make candles, ikons, images and other religious articles. This formal permission would be quite meaningless if necessary materials and labor were not released by the Government.

But the fact is that a Soviet for Church Affairs has been established, directly under the Sovnarkom, or Council of People's Commissars, specifically to review Church requests. The Synod now also has its own printshop, where it publishes the *Magazine of the Moscow Patriarchate,* a full-size illustrated monthly. I met the long-haired editor, who looked like a double for Rasputin, and he told me that his journal circulates, in 10,000 copies, to the clergy throughout the Union. It was said, with what truth I was unable to ascertain, that the magazine received the paper allotment formerly assigned to Yaroslavsky's old Anti-God publication—now defunct.

Nicolai Kurchivsky confirmed the report that many Pioneers

and Komsomols were now coming to church. He said that there was no ban against Komsomol attendance at mass, but he considered that full-fledged Communists still had to reject God, in accordance with materialist philosophy.

"Many army officers attend services," he claimed. "In the recovered areas priests say mass immediately after the Red Army arrives, and often the commander attends, with his staff, whether they are believers or not." There were no chaplains in the Army as yet—the Synod tried hard to get some in—but Nicolai informed me that individual soldiers often came to the priest for blessing, before going to battle, "In the villages special services are held, at the request of parents, before new recruits leave to join the Army."

The Church is now permitted to give instruction to children of the devout, who request it, and catechism classes are regularly held in Moscow cathedrals after the long Orthodox services. Perhaps the greatest concession yet made by the Kremlin was the permission granted to the Church to open the Bogoslavsky Theological Seminary in Moscow, in the old Novodevishi Monastery, founded by the Grand Duke Vassili, in 1525. Students who enter there must be eighteen years old, graduates of Soviet middle schools, believers in the Russian Orthodox faith, and able to read the Slavonic languages. They each receive a stipend of 200 rubles monthly and get "essential worker" rations. Enrollment for the first year was promptly filled.

Nicolai said that the Church heartily approved of the new marriage and divorce laws, particularly the tightening up on divorce. Also, it seemed that enforcement of registered marriages was followed by a wave of church weddings and baptisms. The new law speaks vaguely of "solemnizing weddings," but the Government announced no further details, and many people interpreted this, whether it was so intended or not, to sanction a church ceremony.

A conference of Evangelical Christians and Baptists, with forty-five delegates from all parts of the nation, including Siberia and the liberated areas, was called in Moscow in 1944 and voted to set up an all-Union council of united Christians. Roman Catholics, Jews and Mohammedans are also taking advantage of the conciliatory policy to restore some churches, synagogues and mosques and to increase their following. All these activities come under the government-sponsored Soviet for Church Affairs.

Let no one imagine, however, that the State has made any concession to religion as a separate power or authority in secular life. Atheism is still taught in the schools, and young people, except where parents have been extremely zealous, remain indifferent to the idea of God. Any notion that religious instruction might be be admitted to educational institutions was dispelled by warnings such as the following recently issued to Young Communists: *

"It is no use concealing the fact that among the teachers there are people, a small number it is true, who have recently begun to show tolerance toward religion. Cases of observance of religious ceremonies by teachers have even increased. Our party's attitude toward religion is well known and has not changed. Our party fights against religious prejudices because it stands for science, while all religion is contrary to science.

"By what means does our party fight against religion? M. I. Kalinin gave a good answer to this question in his talk to front-line agitators in 1943. He said, 'We do not persecute anyone for religion. We regard it as an error and fight against it with enlightenment.' In conformity with the requirements of our party, care must be taken to avoid any offense to the feelings of believers, which only leads to a strengthening of religious fanaticism."

Despite the fact that "believers" persist even among the school-teachers, the State can afford to be more tolerant, since the power of the Church to organize resistance has been completely broken. It possesses no important economic power. It

* *Komsomalskaya Pravda*, Sept. 17, 1944.

can in no way control or influence livelihood or threaten the socialist system, nor does it any longer criticize Communism.

The truth is that the Church is no longer "the agency of the former ruling class"; it is the obedient "agency" of the proletarian state. The Government looks upon the Church more benignly now because it can without fear employ it as an organization amenable to its political will, and helpful in the conquest of the last islands of opposition left in the populace.

The Kremlin also fully realizes the usefulness of the Patriarchate and the Synod in reconciling Slav-Orthodox elements in the neighbor states of Rumania, Bulgaria, Yugoslavia, and to a lesser extent in Poland, Czechoslovakia and Hungary, in its struggle against the Vatican for moral ascendancy in Europe.

III

The "New" Education

Nowhere in the new education is the frank attempt to reestablish a connection with the past more evident than in the Suvorov schools, which have sprung up only since the war. At the end of 1944 there were fifteen Suvorov schools and more were to be opened both in the liberated areas and in uninvaded Russia.

First of all, why was the name of Alexander Suvorov honored in these special schools for favored youths? Why not Marx or Lenin or Stalin? Why not any one of a half dozen revolutionary heroes? Suvorov was, of course, the celebrated military genius of Russian history, and the only one who fought a highly successful war deep in Europe. But he is a purely national hero; there is nothing revolutionary about him. In fact, Suvorov served under Catherine the Great and took a leading part in the suppression of the great peasant uprising led by the Don Cossack Emelian Pugachev, a figure of glamor who inspired early Bolsheviks.

It appears that Suvorov was chosen solely because of his military brilliance. When the schools were opened by a special decree of the Sovnarkom, *Red Star* announced that here "the children of the generals and honored officers of the Red Army begin a life career which will forever be linked with the military profession."

"Suvorovtsi," as the young cadets are called, are chosen from among the orphans of Red Army heroes, whether officers or enlisted men and from sons of high officers and ranking party officials. A few older youths who distinguished themselves, on their own, during the war, are also admitted. The schools are not open to the general public. So great is their popularity that there are a hundred times as many aspirants as can be received. In the Suvorov school I visited, at Kalinin, 12,000 applications were received in 1944, and only seventy boys were admitted.

I found the Kalinin school located in a building once used as a seminary, and now commanded by a major-general, one Eremenko, with a teaching staff of officers and a few uniformed women. Students ranged in age from eight to fourteen. It is a boarding school; the state furnishes everything, including the well-tailored uniforms of good black cloth, topped off by a special white-crowned hat. Parents or friends are allowed to visit the cadets twice a week and there is a short vacation. For the rest of the time the Suvorov cadets live under strict military discipline. Uniforms are worn in classes and on the street; the day begins and ends with bugle calls; and military forms of address are compulsory. Cadets go on many excursions, but as a group, led by an officer-teacher.

Suvorov schools "carry out," to quote *Red Star*,* "the best

* Dec. 1, 1943.

traditions of the old Cadet Establishments, where many celebrated officers and generals of the Russian Army began their
careers." The curriculum also closely recalls the famous Tsarist
schools. Music, fencing, riding and dancing, and physical culture and drill, are part of an enlarged curriculum.

In the years following the Revolution the cadet schools, together with stress on dancing and good manners, disappeared.
Now cadets are reminded that "A Russian is a kind son, a trustworthy comrade, a modest well-educated youth, and a patient,
punctual, efficient officer." At the end of the first year of the
"Suvorovtsi," *Red Star* "observed with great satisfaction that
students have become more disciplined, acquired the necessary
military appearance, tidiness and accuracy . . . behaved with dignity and reserve . . . were respectful toward the old and saluted
officers in a military manner."[*] I noticed how in the dining room
even the youngest children are taught table etiquette.

At the dancing classes I watched students struggling hard to
master the steps taught to them by a graceful ballerina. My
secretary was with me that day—the incomparable Anna Erma-
layeva, daughter of a once wealthy Russian merchant.

"Why, good gracious," Anna suddenly exclaimed, "they are
learning the same steps—the Hungarian dance and the *pas-de-
patineurs*—that we used to dance at the balls when I was a girl!"

In the old days entire companies and detachments of cadets
used to go to the seasonal dances at fashionable girls' schools.
Now Major Savresenski, standing beside me, said his cadets had
been invited to several balls to be held in local girls' schools. In
turn, the Suvorov boys were staging a dance to which the girl
students would be invited.

"History's wheel has come full circle!" laughed Anna.

But it is far from full, actually. One has to remember that those
cadets who had won entrance to this exclusive school were mostly
orphans, or the sons of outstanding patriots themselves the offspring of humble peasants. The whole idea was still in an ex-

[*] Sept. 1, 1944.

perimental stage. It was not yet decided how students were to be selected in the future—when the orphan problem—and there were 4,000,000 newly orphaned Russian children—had been solved. There was already a tendency to interpret the schools as preparation for entrance into non-military professions as well as the Army. In classes I questioned some students announced that they intended to become scientists or writers, when they graduated from an eight-year course here.

I was much struck by another thing. I asked a number of cadets why they thought Russia was winning the war. Without exception, they all answered in words to this effect, "Because Germany was the aggressor and our country was invaded. Our people are fighting for their Fatherland against enslavement. Our cause is just." That did not sound as if they were being trained for purposes of conquest or aggression.

In ordinary public schools also great emphasis is now placed on discipline, care for one's parents and respect for elders, officials and officers. Military training begins in the fourth year of primary school. All students are required to stand at attention when answering the teacher's queries, and to march to and from classes in columns wheeling right and left.

"The war," wrote Captain N. I. Boldirev in the authoritative *Soviet Pedagogics*,* "has revealed serious deficiencies in our system of education in general, and in the organization of military training in particular." Boldirev held the school system responsible for the following weaknesses in its human products: 1) lack of will power, obstinacy, hardiness and other moral qualities; 2) lack of military knowledge; 3) absence of a sense of discipline, owing to failure to "demand from pupils absolute obedience to the teacher" and "absolute conformance to the established order"; and 4) lack of development of the "habit of labor."

"It is necessary," declared Boldirev, "to have in mind that even after the war the problem of military training will never lose

* Feb.–March, 1943.

its importance and significance. Comrade Stalin states that the defense of our country is the first function of the socialist state. And since capitalist encirclement exists, our country 'must have a well-trained army to defend the gains of socialism against attacks from without.' "

Much of the increased emphasis on military discipline, however, doubtless grows out of the simple and obvious necessity to recover the ground lost in educational effort during the war and to restore stability to the whole educational system. Thousands of schools were burned or destroyed; thousands of teachers were lost or went int othe Army; and millions of youths of school age received little or no training for several years. Youths from the age of twelve onward were drafted into labor on farms or in factories, to replace their elders, while thousands of others went into Labor Reserve schools where general education was limited.

In the latter part of the war great efforts were made to supplement the interrupted education of working youths. Thousands of night schools were opened in the villages for farmer boys and girls and similar schools were established in big factory districts, to provide the equivalent of full primary and middle-school education. The standard in the work-and-study Labor Reserve schools also was raised, and many became comparable to good vocational training institutes. In three years the Government spent over six billion rubles on Labor Reserve schools alone, where all food and clothing, as well as fairly generous monthly wages for work performed, are furnished by the State. During the war over 2,000,000 young technicians, many of them highly qualified specialists, were trained by this system.

IV

Communism=Patriotism

HAS Russian patriotism, with all its heroes of the bourgeois and feudal past, been permanently enlisted as an ally of the Soviet system, and fully reconciled to the teachings of Marxist internationalism? Well—consider this advice to Communist teachers, from *Komsomolskaya Pravda* ("Young Communist Truth"): *

"The teaching of Russian language and literature must show the universal character of Russian literature and the Russian people, who have produced such literary giants as Pushkin, Lermontov, Tolstoy, Dostoyevski, Turgenev, Gogol, Belinski, Nekrasov, Chernishevski, Chekhov, Gorky, and Mayakovsky. In the teaching of Russian, emphasis must be laid on the profound patriotism of Russian literature.

"The teaching of history must develop in schoolchildren a love for the heroic past of our people, which, throughout the whole of its history, has displayed unexampled bravery, courage, firmness and unity in defending the honor, freedom and independence of its native land. The Russians stopped the Mongols and saved Europe from them. They saved Europe from being enslaved by the French and Napoleon. They have saved the whole world from the bondage of Hitlerite Germany.

"In the teaching of mathematics and the natural sciences emphasis must be laid on the part which Russian scholars such as Lomonosov, Lobachevski, Mendelev, Sechenov, Timiryazov,

* Sept. 17, 1944.

194

Popov, Mechnikov, Tsiolkovski, Michurin, Pavlov, etc., have played in developing them. The teaching of geography must reveal the innumerable resources of our great country and develop in young people a love for its natural features. Love of the country must determine and inspire teachers."

Literature has even performed a face-lifting job on Ivan IV, long popularly known as "The Terrible." The writer of a new novel, V. Kostylev, has shown him to be "the state-builder, the patriot of his time, an experienced politician and a penetrating judge of human motivations and human interests." Ivan was in reality the leader of "the progressive and constructive state cause" against the reactionary feudal *boyars* (regional lords) striving toward a break-up of the state," according to no less an authority than *Pravda*.*

A similar trend has become noticeable in the entire press, in public lectures and in scientific institutions. Last year special conferences were called to draw attention to the contribution to world knowledge of pre-Soviet inventors, scientists and engineers. Some of their claims might not find ready acceptance elsewhere. Among other things, it was asserted that Russians built the steam engine before Watt and invented a carbon filament lamp before Edison's incandescent. They invented the first rotary motor, the first transformer, the first arc lamp, etc.

"Russian scientists," it appears, "derived the creative strength for their scientific and inventive activity from their unbounded love of their country and of the nation."**

All of which has plenty of equivalent in self-praise to be found in most other countries. But while Soviet Russia was in the past never stingy in its use of superlatives, these were generally reserved for post-revolutionary figures. For an entire lecture to be devoted to "the universal historical importance of classical Russian philosophy," as happened in the case of Dr. Ivochuk speaking before the Riga State University in December, 1944, would

---

* Dec. 11, 1944.
** *Vechernaya Moskva*, Nov. 28, 1944.

hardly have been possible in days when every philosophical concept contemporary with Marx or his disciples, but contradictory in content, was held in anathema, and when everything good about Soviet society had to have its Bolshevik originators.

But it would be a serious mistake to conclude that Soviet Marxism is on the decline, or that the new glorification of Russia's past means a return to the old economic and political system. Far from it. These tendencies seem to indicate the party's increased self-confidence and sense of stability. The party is no longer afraid that acknowledgment of those roots can wither the tree of socialism itself, or transform it again into a tree of bourgeois-capitalist reaction. Rather, in the indestructible cultural heritage of the nation it now sees vital roots of society which can help nourish and protect its own system.

The Communists have frankly decided to identify their own leadership with the full flowering of all that was best in Great Russian nationalism, and to make it, too, an "agency of the new ruling class, the proletariat," while retaining all the basic teachings of Soviet Marxism.

CHAPTER TWELVE

The Party and the People

····◦】【◦·····

I

Morality and Soviet Politics

PRESENT efforts of the party, then, center on the complex tasks of synchronizing and synthesizing "local" patriotism with Marxism, and Russian nationalism with the Soviet policy of national and racial equality. Owing to preoccupation with primary military problems, the loss of thousands of the best party cadres in battle, the disorganization of the party apparatus in the occupied areas, and the greatly increased importance of women and 'teen-age youth in industry and agriculture, Marxist training deteriorated in the early war years. In 1944 there began an intensified new drive to indoctrinate masses of "political illiterates," to combat the effects of Nazi propaganda, and to train Red Army men and Young Communists to fill up the party ranks.

"Particular attention must be devoted to explaining the role of the Soviet State, the Bolshevik Party and the friendship of the peoples of the USSR as the major factors which have secured for our country victory over the German fascist aggressors," declared a party plenum held in Moscow in October, 1944. "Our propagandists must emphasize the distinctiveness of this war from all other wars of liberation, for in it is being defended not only the national independence of the Soviet Union but also the conquests of the Great October Socialist Revolution. It is necessary to educate the masses in the spirit of Leninist-Stalinist internationalism, in the spirit of the friendship of the peoples of the USSR."

197

Everywhere and in every way, now, the people are reminded that they have been victorious because the great party of Lenin and Stalin was there to lead the nation. "The Bolsheviks have ennobled the idea of patriotism and raised it to an unprecedented height. The Bolsheviks have brought into the battle countless masses of people conscious of their responsibility for the fate of their country. The Russian people has always shown breadth of spirit in its deeds in the historical arena, but in our day it has not only evoked the tradition of the past but has shown a new character, hitherto unknown to the world."*

Stalin's speeches *On the Patriotic War* and the Stalin-edited *Short Course History of the Communist Party of the Soviet Union* (and articles in the party papers and journals which paraphrase or quote from them) are the basic materials for the new mass political education and re-education. From fighters at the front to youthful workers in the rear, even down to Pioneers and Timurs, extracts from those texts are being drilled into the people and committed to memory. Regiments in the battle line had their "Mobile Party Cabinet" and frequent lectures "aimed to bring about concrete military results." Party propagandists in such work appeared beside tables covered with red cloth on which are laid out periodicals and pamphlets where soldiers come for guidance, as to a chaplain.

Intellectuals and scientists are exhorted to master Marxism, "science of the sciences." Even ballet girls in the Bolshoi Theater have to learn their party catechism and pass examinations on the teachings of Stalin. Russian art, we are told by Comrade Solodovnikov in *Bolshevik,** also draws its greatness from both the unbounded love of the artist for his country and the Soviet power. While "with the decay of capitalism the art of ruling classes in the bourgeois countries has been ever withdrawing from life, from great problems, and ... inaccessible for the broad masses," under the hegemony of victorious socialism have come "the conditions necessary for the development of art really free

* *Red Star*, Sept. 15, 1944.

and serving tens of millions of toilers . . . Ideology, patriotic expediency and realistic tendencies have become organic qualities of Soviet art. These qualities differ from bourgeois art and make it the most advanced in the world."

Solodovnikov issues a warning to the "art for art's sakers," those who misuse patriotism as a cloak to glorify reactionary figures. "Drama, painting, song—all these are also means of propaganda and agitation carried on through artistic images and for this reason more accessible to the masses and deep in their penetration. Hence it is clear how important it is for art to be a party, a Bolshevist, art."

Morality, too, is said to reach its highest development in a new combination of historic virtues of the Russian people with Soviet ideology. During the war years Stalin more and more used the word "morality" and the party gave it new definitions. "Moral and political unity," says Stalin, "is the great motive pov. ¬ of our society." In a public lecture in Moscow, Professor M. P. Baskin recently announced that the "moral qualities of the Soviet people lie in their daring, courage, patriotism, love for the father-land, love for the party, for the cause of Lenin and Stalin." To these he added Soviet promotion of family love, of loyalty in personal relationships, of rejection of the idea of "free love," and of the moral rectitude of party leaders. All such qualities are rooted in Bolshevik leadership, for "there is no morality outside of politics."

---·❦ ❧·---

II

Rebuilding the Party

A VAST new crop of party functionaries is now receiving its training, particularly in the Army and in the former occupied areas, where war and the tests of war wiped out Communists by the thousands, if not the millions. In the Ukraine, in the Crimea, in White Russia and the Baltic states, the old party machine was subjected to terrific stress and in many districts it collapsed.

In the case of the Crimea, homeland of the Tartars and their autonomous republic, the moral failure" was so pronounced that the TSEKA issued a special admonition to party leaders, from which critical lessons were drawn throughout the country. Tartar-born Communists were accused of having neglected Marxist education of their people and of distorting party teachings. False "Tartar nationalism" had been preached. The truth of the matter was that many Tartars welcomed the Germans who promised them independence, and that in the Crimea no effective guerrilla warfare was ever organized. Thousands of backsliding Tartars were therefore exiled from the Crimea, and at one time the TSEKA was rumored to be seriously considered abolishing the autonomous Tartar Republic altogether.

Nationalists in the Ukraine, too, often proved more influential with the inhabitants than the Communist cadres left behind to organize resistance. Thousands of Ukrainians were killed in a scattered behind-the-lines civil war, led by imported "White" Ukrainians and backed by the Germans. For a time the party seemed likely to lose its influence over the whole countryside.

200

In Kiev, the Ukrainian capital, I talked with V. F. Starchenko, a member of the TSEKA, and vice-chairman of the Ukrainian Government, about the extent of the Nazi imprint left on the party and the people. This cool, efficient, realistic, young man admitted that Communist leaders had at one time been quite concerned, but said that the problem of counter-education was minimized owing largely to the German's own greed and political ineptitude. They had, he claimed, in the end done most of the Russians' great job for them, by alienating all potential Ukranian sympathizers through a policy of indiscriminate looting, destruction and atrocity.

"We have been making a detailed study of German methods," said Starchenko, "and we have concluded that no central plan was ever carried out, either economically or p litically. In a few districts the Germans did divide the land; ut then they took away almost the entire crop. In other plac s German civilians were given land and the peasants were mad serfs. In most cases the collectives were never dissolved. In some places the peasants were told they could elect their own *starotsi*, or village chiefs, but they refused to do so, or the *starotsi* would decline to take office after the election. The policy varied according to the army commandant. About the only Ukrainians who were given any authority were some of the old 'Whites' in exile, who came back with the Nazi troops."

The real reason for the Germans' failure apparently was that in the beginning they were confident they would be in the Ukraine forever and they didn't care what the people thought. In this period their greed and arrogance were excessive. They took the best land for German settlers and robbed other farms of their best cattle, their machinery and their surplus and reserves. Meanwhile able-bodied girls and boys over thirteen were conscripted and sent to forced labor in Germany. Over this system the Nazis set up a few Ukrainian-German or Ukrainian-Polish puppets, whose appeals to Ukrainian nationalism soon fell on deaf ears in view of the circumstances. Many of the puppets themselves were killed by partisans or assassinated by the peasants, more and more of whom took to the forests. Gestapo and SS troops carried out so many atrocities, also, that even the most anti-Soviet peasants were outraged. When, finally, the Germans began to see that they needed the people to help fight the Red Army, it was far too late. The Nazi repression thus won acceptance for the Bolshevik alternative to a degree never attained before the war.

Nevertheless, difficulties of replacing party personnel in the Ukraine and developing people competent to carry on the ideological reconstruction work there were very severe. Party practice was to draw chiefly on the Army and on youths who had actively demonstrated their anti-Nazi feelings by joining the partisans. In Kiev, I learned that out of 1,438 secretaries of local Komsomol organizations, for example, 1,437 had been Young Communists less than four months. In Kharkov oblast 313 Komsomol secretaries were changed in 1944, and fifty-two party secretaries. In many places ninety-five percent of the party members disappeared during the war or were expunged from the rolls.

A young Komsomol leader sent by Moscow headquarters to reorganize the party and conduct counter-propaganda in the Donbas told me some very interesting things about her work there. She said that the German occupation had left only hatred and disgust for the Nazi system in the majority of the people. They had failed to win any significant following on the basis of such private capitalism as they had permitted to revive. Both workers and farmers were actually much worse off, materially, under the Germans, than they had been in the last years of the Soviets, and so many features of their cultural life had been destroyed that, in retrospect, the Soviet period began to seem like a golden era.

"But in one respect," this girl told me, "the Nazis did succeed in corrupting some of our people. That was by their anti-Semitic propaganda. After three years of Nazi occupation, and constant propaganda against the Jews, without any educational effort or information to combat it, some people were poisoned. One of our hardest tasks is to combat this."

Nazi anti-Semitic ideology tended to have some effect on Red Army men, also; the usual stories against the Jews circulated to some extent among civilians, and one heard occasional complaints against discrimination. Soviet propaganda combated this by publishing facts about tens of thousands of Jewish officers and men and Communist Party workers, killed or wounded or decorated in battle. The Constitutional law against advocacy of racial hatred was strictly enforced whenever action was brought against such slanderers. On one occasion the head of the Soviet Propaganda Bureau, A. S. Shcherbakov, made a radio broadcast threatening stern measures to stamp out any signs of Nazi-inspired race prejudice.

But while no quarter was given to anti-Semitic sentiments, nor to any revival of private enterprise, the Kremlin appeared more impressed with Ukrainian and White Russian nationalist aspirations. In any case, the decree of 1943, promising wider autonomy to the various republics, met great popularity in these two most important European nations of the Soviet Union. It was followed by increased emphasis on the independent role of Ukrainian and White Russian peoples and their history and culture, in the building of socialism and in the defense of the USSR. Some critics abroad professed to see in the appointment of separate foreign ministers for the Ukraine and White Russia only a subtle Kremlin move to provide a pattern to simplify future annexations of border states, or to get extra votes in the new world peace organizations. While such ideas may possibly have influenced the decision, the consensus among informed foreigners in Moscow was that it was far more likely due primarily to internal political considerations and especially to the Kremlin's desire to ally to itself the immense enthusiasm which the war-proved "local" national patriotism can still evoke.

III

Criticism

THERE is a widespread assumption in America and Britain that because freedom of speech, press, assembly and organization does not exist in Russia, in our sense, there is no such thing as public opinion or public or private criticism. If that were the case then there would be serious danger of an ever-widening gulf between government and people, until the rulers would presently be as remote as the Tsar was. Underground forces could then gather and assume explosive proportions before compromise measures could be enforced to divide the opposition.

The fact is, however, that public opinion does exist in Russia, and made itself felt during the war, in many overt and covert ways. First of all, remember that all Russia's present high officials themselves rose from the peasantry or the working class. Many still consciously identify themselves with the peasants, even in their living habits; and all of them, subconsciously, react with the mentality of their own class toward given situations. Men like Kalinin and Andreyev, who spent their youth working in the village fields, and men like Voroshilov and Malenkov, who toiled over machines, probably do not need a ballot to tell them how the people feel about the way things are.

Secondly, there *is*, or at least is encouraged to be, a great deal of freedom of expression in local affairs. Collective farm villages do elect their own officers, and unpopular ones can be so easily sabotaged and ruined by the peasants that a party-dictated choice can seldom "stick." This applies also to local soviets, which carry a lot of responsibility. Many local and even district non-party officials are elected to office—although in practice the machinery of the party is, of course, sufficiently potent and omnipresent to exclude any man or woman from office by withholding its support.

Beyond the purely local soviet, however, most officials are straight-out party candidates. The difference between the election of a public official to higher office in Russia, and one in the United States, is that there is no opposition *party* candidate; all potential office-seekers must represent faith in one ideology, one system, and adherence to one central social and economic plan handed down from above—which they can influence only infinitesimally. In fairness it must be admitted, however, that the some five million Communists, and fifteen million Young Communists, probably represent a larger percentage of ϫtal population than the active membership of any single party in u. United States—especially when it is remembered that each ot ϫhose party members is expected closely to influence two or three nonparty people in the general public, and be able to call them loyal followers. In that way, it can be seen, the party sends out antennae to all corners of the country and all sections of the population.

But since in Russia the threat of a legal *party* opposition does not arise, the "sense of responsibility" of the ruling power must be largely self-imposed. Thus you get the extraordinary phenomenon of a party in power becoming its own sole effective critic. And since it is impossible to draw a sharp line separating the state administrative apparatus from the party, this means that the Government also must be its own critic. For this purpose special party-control commissions, as well as governmental commissions, are established to express critical opinion and make it effective.

Thus, side by side with all the self-praise and glorification I have mentioned, the Soviet press throughout the war carried sharp criticisms of party and state officials. Over a period of months I collected literally hundreds of items of this nature, covering a wide variety of activity. Probably the most numerous reprimands and warnings were addressed to officials responsible for weaknesses in the production system.

Slipshod methods of harvesting, which resulted in great losses of grain, were continuously criticized in specific regions. Individual officials caught in the wrongful use or appropriation of state property were singled out as examples. Instances of losses due to poor packing and shipment of manufactured goods were frequently cited, and engineers responsible for waste of metals and materials were upbraided. Outright thefts of materials and embezzlement of funds were exposed and cases of bribery of state employees were frequently reported in the Government and party press.

Blockheadedness, indifference to duty, and evasion of responsibility by officials and bureaucrats were the subject of many editorials and newspaper stories, in which individuals and localities were often mentioned by name. The detail into which these criticisms enter is frequently surprising. One long article in *Pravda*, for example, was devoted to ridiculing the chairman of the Vologda Soviet for refusing to permit the marriage bureau to buy a new set of curtains and to separate it from the funeral bureau. The writer concluded that the "hearts of the administrators of Vologda" were made of gristle.

An article of similar length in the great national newspaper, *Izvestia*, was devoted to denouncing the town of Chelyabinsk for not making better layettes for babies, and for producing "nothing but goods of trashy quality for children." From Ryazan a *Pravda* correspondent reported that no layettes at all were provided by the town authorities and that the local maternity home had been forced to buy two second-hand layettes from a government commission store—the equivalent of a pawn shop. Other town fathers were rebuked for failing to provide adequate living quarters, for inhuman bureaucracy, for falsifying reports, for neglecting improvements in the school system, and so on.

One could be fairly sure that, in every instance when such scandals reached the point where publicity was given to them, numerous complaints from the people had filtered through to higher control organizations, had brought on investigation, and would doubtless be followed promptly by punishment of those responsible. Open criticism of different party branches for failure to accomplish their educational and organizational duties, in the rear and at the front, also, usually preceded or coincided with dismissals and new appointments. And from the extent of such criticism in the press it was evident that a process of change and reform was going on all the time.

Indeed, if this self-criticism permeated the higher organs of the Government to the same degree which was evident outside Moscow, one might have concluded that no more efficient a system for enforcing responsiveness to public opinion existed. No doubt much vigilance was exercised in closed sessions of the higher party organs, but it was quite noticeable that at the level of all-union commissariats of the Government, where some of the worst bureaucratic abuses existed, virtually no criticism appeared in print.

In the Commissariat for Foreign Affairs, as an outstanding example most familiar to foreign correspondents, the Press Department and all the Soviet agencies responsible for the conduct of foreign propaganda provided daily instances of inefficiency, which often amounted to sabotage of the war effort. But no word of criticism of any propaganda official or bureaucrat ever crept into the press. The Sovinformburo, a big organization with millions of rubles to spend, was in its operations in English-speaking countries undoubtedly the least effective branch of the Government from the standpoint of results obtained in relation to time and money spent. Yet its worst mistakes remained uncorrected—and apparently internally uncriticized—throughout the war.

In no way was the obtuseness of the Soviet propaganda policy with Allied and friendly countries more evident than in its treatment of foreign correspondents. The Press Department, to whom all correspondents are accredited, apparently frankly took the line that the less correspondents saw of the people and their organizations, the better it would be for Russia. Weeks of negotiation were often required even before a correspondent could visit a school, and trips to the front were arranged only as conducted affairs. No group of correspondents in the world exhibited greater patience and restraint under the conditions imposed, and demonstrated greater industry and ingenuity in breaking out of the isolation to which they were condemned.

For the net result of the Press Department's policy was not to prevent correspondents from getting acquainted with Russians or learning about Soviet life. The more industrious learned the language sufficiently to operate on their own, and more and more ignored the Press Department in seeking contacts and information. And it was these Russian people, whom one met in spite of the official policy, who gave the correspondent his impression of the country and the attitude of the public toward the Government.

One of the surprising discoveries you make, once you break away from the Foreign Office atmosphere of frustration and bureaucracy, is the degree of freedom with which the Russian speaks about everything with his friends. I have heard no more severe criticism of the Soviet Government than from Russians themselves, and sometimes even from party members. But at the same time the most effective "propagandizing" ever done on me has been through contacts with ordinary Russians who conceded the good things accomplished by their Government, along with their criticism of the bad. It was most effective simply because it proved that beneath all the system of controls the individual Russian still had a mind of his own and still spoke his opinions in private with a freedom that gave reality to the existence of criticism. In this way one was able to form a judgment of the achievements of the Soviet system and dispel a good deal of the skepticism which one naturally felt for self-praise produced by the propaganda bureau.

IV

The Door to Russia

So FAR I have emphasized the cultural and psychological effects of war on Soviet society, but on the few remaining pages I want to discuss the influence of war on Soviet foreign policy. As most people know, the richest part of the Soviet Union was laid waste during these years. Decades of hard work lie ahead to restore the devastated areas. This work has to be accomplished by a people physically worn-out after almost intolerable toil. It has to be done largely by women and children and old people—and as much of the able-bodied manpower as returns intact out of an army that mobilized approximately 30,000,000 men to throw into the maw of war.

This experience will never be forgotten by the Soviet Government. It knows that another great war would mean total extinction for the defeated races and nations. The Russians will take every measure necessary to prevent any combination from arising again, in Europe or Asia, which can repeat an invasion.

On the other hand, the Russian people are not militaristic; they are not aggressive-minded. They are conscious of their vast spaces and depleted population and they do not consciously want more territory. Most observers in Russia also think that the Communist leaders do not want—or will not dare to run the risks of—expansion just for ideological reasons. But they still distrust and fear the kind of Europe that has bred generations of war-makers. They fear insecurity more than we do because they have not got two oceans nor even an English channel protecting them. If the last two wars had cost us over 30,000,000 military and civilian casualties, as they have cost the peoples of Russia, we would doubtless take measures no less decisive than those they demand, to immunize our frontiers against another potential invader.

On the whole it still seems correct to say that the main purpose of all Soviet foreign policy is to safeguard the nation against attack, so that in the years ahead the people can realize, with their own resources, a life as prosperous and happy as our own. It was, after all, Soviet diplomats who first insisted that "peace is indivisible" and demanded "collective security." But their leaders often make mistakes in the way they try to achieve se-curity. Their ideas of the causes of war are different from ours, and in trying to eliminate them they often needlessly arouse distrust and suspicion abroad.

It must be remembered, however, that all the responsible Soviet leaders believed in the idea of "capitalist encirclement" before this war and that this notion is not dead, despite the un-expected turn of events. For that reason, because the Russians identify European landlords and capitalists with "fascist" war-making forces, and because in truth they do not know how to assist any other kind of society to function, the impact of the Red Army wherever it goes inevitably results in laying the basis for "pre-socialist" states. But that Stalin has any desire to start a general civil war to "bolshevize" Europe, or to annex new ter-ritories, or any adventure that might lead to a new great war is not credible to one familiar with the invalided condition of his country. Certainly no one who has lived in Russia during this war, and seen the price the nation has paid for survival, can doubt the sincerity or the profound need behind the Soviet demand for as long a peace as the world can arrange.

We now think of Russia as a "mighty nation," and in terms of victory it is. But its leaders know that in truth it is now weak and exhausted. Paradoxically, a consciousness of vulnerability often lies behind many Soviet moves in Eastern Europe which are here considered aggressive and growing out of a new sense of power. But let no one be fooled; the Kremlin and the Russian people are both fully aware of the importance of American Lend-Lease aid in helping them to survive. And they are both fully conscious of the necessity for continued post-war aid on almost as big a scale. If our diplomacy with Russia has been ineffective, it is because we have not stated our political aims with clarity and conciseness in a manner which the Russians could consider as a serious alternative to their methods of establishing stability and security, nor as a *quid pro quo* for our present and future aid.

Russia has been heavily dependent on us, and continues to be, but historical and geographical factors predetermined that, and it does not follow that the Soviet economic system proved weak. On the contrary, it demonstrated remarkable flexibility and adaptability, most observers in Russia agree. We have already seen how, despite the huge damage to the most advanced areas, the pre-war volume of industrial production for the country as a whole was actually recovered in many respects in 1944. A system capable of recovery under such handicaps will certainly meet the post-war needs of its people.

I hope no one gets the idea that I mean to say Russia has attained anything like the development and standard of living of our country. It is still very, very far behind us. But the important fact is that the Russians were beginning to get the food and clothing they needed, in the two years before this war. They have not forgotten that. Their cultural life had been enormously enriched, also, compared to their own past—the fairest yardstick of progress for any country. People who have been studying Russia pretty closely now agree that, if helped by American machinery imports, the Soviet Union will probably surpass its pre-war production of industrial and agricultural goods within this decade. Russians have good reason to believe that ten years from today, when the Ukraine has been fully restored, their people will be enjoying a higher mass living standard than any nation on the continent of Europe or Asia.

Once that becomes a fact, but *only then*, and once the Kremlin feels reasonably secure in a peaceful world, it may become possible for the Russian people to enjoy the freedoms of political democracy—a democracy more in line with our own best traditions—side by side with the Soviet system of economy. Until then, the doors between Russia and the advanced capitalistic countries will not fully open. But now they are at least ajar. It is our responsibility, as much as it is Russia's, to see that they are not again slammed shut.

Madison, Conn.
April, 1945.